AFRICAN REALITIES

AFRICAN REALITIES
A MEMOIR

ROBINSON M NABULYATO

edited by GIACOMO MACOLA
with a forward by BIZECK J PHIRI

The Lembani Trust
LUSAKA

http://sites.google.com/site/lembanitrust/

Published in 2008 by the Lembani Trust
Lusaka, Zambia

Copyright © 2009 the estate of Robinson M Nabulyato

All rights reserved. Except for brief quotations in a review, this book, or any part thereof, may not be reproduced, stored into or introduced into a retrieval system, or transmitted, in any form or by any means, electronic, mechanical, photocopying, recording, or otherwise, without the written permission of the copyright owner.

ISBN 978-9982-9972-0-1

Cover and book design by Lawrence Dritsas

To my dear wife, Marian,
And to our children,
Kaambwa (Joyce), Shakopa (Godfrey),
Mwashintambo (Patrick), Shikalimbwe (Ernest),
Shikatuba (Austin) and Shandumba (Francis).

Contents

Foreword..x
Editor's Introduction..xiii
Author's Preface...xx

1 Early Life...1

2 My School Days and Teaching Career...8

3 The Roots of my Political Career...15

4 Joining Forces with Some Other People....................................20

5 Congress Goes to the Districts..26

6 Congress Delegations to London..31

7 Africans in the Legislative Council of Northern Rhodesia...................36

8 From the Split in the African National Congress to Independence....41

9 Invitation to Take Up the Speakership.....................................45

10 Parliamentary Government vs. Dictatorship.........................51

12 The Spirit of Self-Help and Sacrifice in Zambia and Africa...............63

13 The Economic and Political Future of Africa.........................71

14 Threats to Democracy in Africa..79

Documents

1: Nabulyato on Marcus Garvey..9
2: Chalimbana, 1942-1944..10
3: Nabulyato on the Missionaries..12
4: Nabulyato and Colonial Racism...18
5: The Northern Rhodesia African Congress...22
6: Nabulyato's First Visit to the United Kingdom...................................32
7: Fighting Harry Nkumbula in the National Assembly and in Court. 48
8: Nabulyato on the Role of Parliament..60
9: Nabulyato on the Leadership Code...65
10: Human Rights' Abuses in Zambia in the 1980s 69
12: Nabulyato on the Risk of a Military Coup in Zambia.......................80

FOREWORD

by Professor Bizeck J. Phiri

African Realities: A Memoir is a personal account of the life and times of Dr Robinson Mwaakwe Nabulyato, one of the founding fathers of Zambian politics who stood shoulder to shoulder with his fellow freedom fighters. The publication of these memoirs at this stage is more than welcome. Dr Nabulyato distinguished himself as Speaker of the National Assembly of Zambia. African parliaments (Zambia's most prominently) are generally not visible in the body of literature about the continent's politics. *African Realities* is in this respect filling a gap that has been visible in the historiography of Zambia.

Dr Nabulyato served as the fourth (1969-1988) and sixth (1991-1998) Speaker of the National Assembly of Zambia. Nabulyato is the only one with the enviable record of having served as Speaker in all three republics. He served in the latter part of the First republic, during the Second Republic and seven years into the Third Republic. Political observers and commentators have suggested that during the Second Republic Speaker Nabulyato shaped the Zambian Parliament into a true people's parliament. He not only allowed serious criticism of government policy by backbenchers, but also protected the Members' right to speak freely in the House. For example, in a landmark ruling in 1978, he stated that Members of Parliament were free to debate any issue because they spoke on behalf of the electorate. He further added that 'there was no limit to freedom of speech, except by the House itself.'

He was not afraid to make rulings that sometimes embarrassed, or even irritated the Central Committee of the United National Independence Party. He is remembered for banning the use of the term 'comrade' in Parliament describing it as an unparliamentarily and as a 'dirty word'. He earned the name or title of 'Mr Discipline' because of his strict demand for discipline among Members of Parliament. He is the only one to have served twice as Speaker in the history of the Zambian Parliament. He is also remembered for protecting the independence of Parliament from the Judiciary. Once, he was served with a summons from the High Court when Members of the Opposition sued the Speaker. He refused to accept the summons and instructed that the Sheriff who wanted to serve the summons be locked up. He later ordered the release of the Sheriff and the hearing went ahead without his presence. He equally stopped the Attorney General from representing him, because, he maintained, the High Court had made a mistake by accepting a case from the Opposition Party against the Speaker.

Nabulyato's performance as Speaker during the First and Second Republics was very outstanding. Consequently, the first Parliament of the Third Republic re-elected him as Speaker. However, by this time, Nabulyato was generally perceived to be old and out of touch with the political developments and realities of the 1990s. Having been in parliamentary politics for almost a quarter of a century, he was really a political dinosaur. His handling of parliamentary debates and his rulings disappointed many political analysts. Some Members of Parliament accused him of being partial and favouring the ruling Movement for Multiparty Democracy (MMD). He was perceived as being unfit as the Speaker of a House with several political parties. He was accused of exhibiting political traits characteristic of the one-party state era.

Speaker Nabulyato was sometimes accused of making rulings that were unpopular and that led to some Members of Parliament questioning his understanding of the autonomy of the National Assembly. This was particularly the case when he ordered the arrest and detention of columnist Lucy Sichone and Post Newspapers editors Fred M'membe and Bright Mwape for criticising the House. The order was ruled unconstitutional by the High Court. Meanwhile, Akashambatwa Mbikusita Lewanika was on 22 May 1996 expelled from Parliament for disassociating himself from a decision of the National Assembly to indefinitely jail the two journalists. He later sued the Speaker and Justice

Ireen Mambilima ruled that the expulsion was *ultra vires* under Section 8 of the Parliamentary Act. When another opposition MP, Dingiswayo Banda, the Leader of the Opposition, accused Speaker Nabulyato of favouring the ruling party, MMD, he was suspended from the House.

These rulings increasingly raised questions about the Speaker's impartiality and ability successfully to discharge his duty of defending the autonomy of the National Assembly *vis-à-vis* the other arms of government. Nabulyato's last days in Parliament were characterized by controversy attributed to old age and the changed political environment. He retired in 1998 and was replaced by Amusaa Mwanamwambwa.

African Realities certainly provides answers to questions raised and also makes a timely contribution to the historiography on the political evolution of the institution of parliament in Zambia. This book is certainly a must-read for those interested in the politics and parliaments of developing countries. There is a sense in which these memoirs reveal Speaker Nabulyato's perceptive understanding of the value of parliament as an institution that reflects the political dispensation of a country. *African Realities* also illustrates in a unique way the background to the parliamentary reforms that were undertaken long after Speaker Nabulyato was gone. In this respect, the book will help generate more research on the institution of parliament in Zambia.

EDITOR'S INTRODUCTION

Robinson Mwaakwe Nabulyato, most Zambian readers will readily agree, was one of the few true giants of Zambian politics in the twentieth century. A high-ranking Methodist teacher, Nabulyato served as the first General Secretary of the Northern Rhodesia African Congress (Northern Rhodesia African National Congress [ANC] from 1951) between 1948, the year of the party's inception, and 1953, when he was replaced by Kenneth D. Kaunda, independent Zambia's future first Republican President. After relinquishing his seat in the National Executive of the Congress, Nabulyato, who had in the meantime resigned from his teaching post in the Kafue Training Institute and inaugurated a successful retail shop in Banamwaze, his home village in the Namwala district, was nominated to the Ila Native Authority Council and the Southern Province's African Provincial Council, which immediately elected him to the colony-wide African Representative Council. Early in 1954, Nabulyato became one of the four African Members of the Legislative Council (MLCs) of Northern Rhodesia. In 1959, he took part as an Independent in the elections to the Legislative Council (LegCo), but lost to Harry Mwaanga Nkumbula, the ANC's National President and candidate in the South-Western Constituency.

Thereafter, and even though he joined the United National Independence Party (UNIP) between 1959 and 1960, Nabulyato left the Zambian national political scene for close to a decade. His retirement from active politics was brought to an end at the beginning of 1969, when President Kaunda appointed him Speaker of the Zambian National Assembly, a position which he held uninterruptedly until the latter part of 1988, by which time Nabulyato had begun clearly to distance himself from the moribund UNIP one-party regime. The rise and electoral triumph of the Movement for Multi-Party Democracy

(MMD) in 1991 revived yet once more the political fortunes of the 75-year-old Nabulyato. Reinstated to the Chair of the National Assembly, Nabulyato played a dominant role in the early years of the Zambian Third Republic. Old age finally took its toll in 1998, when Nabulyato was forced by ill health to leave a Parliament over which he had towered for nearly thirty years. But life was obviously very dear to Robinson, who battled against numerous crippling infirmities for several more years, exhaling his last breath in as late as September 2004, aged 87.

As stated by the author himself, the bulk of *African Realities* was written in 1988, presumably during the difficult weeks that followed his resignation from the Speakership in November. However, due to numerous misadventures with both local and international publishers, the volume never saw the light of the day during Nabulyato's lifetime. It was only in 2004 that the original typescript was 'rediscovered' among the late Robinson's possessions by his son, Godfrey, who had generously agreed to donate his father's extensive personal documentary collection to the National Archives of Zambia (NAZ), to which the editor was then attached.

Robinson's draft, available for consultation at the NAZ, consists of approximately two-hundred neatly typed pages subdivided into sixteen chapters.[1] These can be usefully conceived of as falling into two separate parts of roughly the same length: an autobiographical section (chapters 1 to 9), followed by a more explicitly analytical part (chapters 10-12, 14-17), dealing mainly with the trajectory of parliamentary democracy in post-colonial Africa and presenting Nabulyato's altogether gloomy appraisal of the continent's future perspectives. While chapters 1 to 9 have been retained in the order and with the titles attributed to them by the late author, the last original seven chapters have been reduced to five, all of which now bear slightly different titles from Nabulyato's. Chapters 10 to 14 of the published version of *African Realities* offer a *bricolage* of the best and most provoking sections of the typescript's

---

[1] The contents page of Nabulyato's typescript, however, suggests that an additional chapter (numbered '13') had once formed part of the text. Entitled 'Democracy and Development in One Party System', this appears to have been irretrievably lost.

documents (i.e. not destined for publication) reproduced in boxes 9 and 12.

When writing about economic polices, a subject on which debate was, if not encouraged, at least tolerated, Nabulyato could afford to be more upfront. By openly defending the principle of free enterprise and the right of individuals to aspire to self-enrichment (chapters 12 and 13), or by pointing out that, far from removing inequality, nationalized economies had merely served to consolidate 'the position of privileged minorities who enjoy plenty in the midst of mass deprivation' (p. 105), Nabulyato was clearly throwing his weight behind the arguments and agenda of a business community whose interests the party in power was proving less and less able to accommodate. Thus, being closely intertwined with the circumstances and context of its compilation, Nabulyato's account offers an informed, insider view of the crisis of an autocratic regime that far too many Zambians have today wrapped in a nostalgic cloud shorn of its multiple failures and deodorized of its most repugnant authoritarian characters.[7]

***

I have said some hard things about Robinson Nabulyato in this introduction. I therefore wish to conclude these brief notes by expressing my most sincere thanks to Mr. Godfrey Nabulyato. Not only did he commission and sponsor the publication of this book, but also, and much more importantly, never sought to hamper my editorial freedom or turn this volume into a glib panegyric. Zambian contemporary memorialists and – may I say it? – political leaders have much to learn from such an honest and self-critical approach to the past.

> Giacomo Macola
> *Lusaka*
> June 2007

---

[7] For a useful definition of autocracy, with special reference to Zambia, see B.J. Phiri, 'Colonial Legacy and the Role of Society in the Creation and Demise of Autocracy in Zambia, 1964-1991', *Nordic Journal of African Studies*, X, 2 (2001), 224-244, esp. 225.

AUTHOR'S PREFACE

I have been pressed by several friends and others to write an account of my experiences as Speaker of the Zambian National Assembly and my observations of political, economic, historical and social changes in Zambia and the world as a whole. In response, I write with no literary pretensions, but with an honest desire to faithfully describe events as I have witnessed them. The decision about what to include and what to omit has been a difficult one, as I have had to keep within reasonable limits the mass of information available to me.

I am immensely indebted to my wife, Marian, for her patience, endurance and forbearance throughout all the years of my public life. I am also deeply grateful to Mr. Ng'oma Mwelwa Chibesakunda, Clerk of the National Assembly, for reading this manuscript and making invaluable corrections. My Secretary, Mrs. Anne Mwila Kasonde, typed and retyped the manuscript with great patience. Both the Clerk of the National Assembly and my Secretary have always given me close assistance and unfailing support. Words fail me to express my gratitude.

I am also conscious of what I owe to all those who have been members of Parliament during my term of office as Speaker from November 1968. Zambians are wonderful people. Even when debating hotly in the House, they always obeyed my orders to calm down. This made my work bearable. All of the National Assembly's members of staff have also played an important role in jettisoning the heavy burden of my work. All in all, it could not have been any better.

CHAPTER 1
Early Life

I was born on 28 October 1916 at Banamwaze village, in the Namwala district of the Southern Province of present-day Zambia (then the British colony of Northern Rhodesia). I am the first born of my mother Nanja (daughter of Senior Headman Shakopa) and my father Shintongo Nabulyato (son of Senior Headman Mwanakwale, shortened to Mwaakwe). My parents were married in 1913, one year before the outbreak of the First World War. Both of my parents were illiterate, but my date of birth was noted down by a European District Officer who had come from the Namwala boma to Banamwaze to recruit soldiers. My birth also coincided with the death of Chief Mukobela (Shekandi) of Baambwe, one of the largest Ila communities in Namwala.

After I was born, my father was recruited into the British Military Forces, first, as a carrier, and, later, as a soldier. I therefore spent my early childhood with my matrilineal uncle Shikalimbwe Shakopa, my mother's elder brother. In those days, the main concern of young Ila boys was to look after cattle. I was no exception to it. My uncle was an enterprising man. He was the first in his area to use a plough pulled by 4 oxen. He was able to do this thanks to the help of two of his Lozi friends, Mubita and Katumwe, who had settled in Shakopa's village after travelling to South Africa and learning the art of taming oxen while working on European farms near Johannesburg. When the oxen had been tamed and a plough purchased, my uncle was so happy that he composed a song in Chiila in praise of his two friends. One of my uncle's oxen was named 'Maachi', after the name of his matrilineal grandfather. The English translation of my uncle's song reads as follows:

> Katumwe bring yokes
> Inspan Maachi, the beautiful ox
> Mubita bring yokes
> Inspan Maachi, the beautiful ox

In the late 1910s, my uncle's deed was rare, though today, in 1988, the plough is commonly used throughout the Southern Province.

Eventually, my uncle's health started to deteriorate. When he realised he was about to die, and since he had no other son, he made me the heir of all of his property. I was even to inherit my uncle's wife, an aunt! That was ridiculous. My uncle Shikalimbwe Shakopa died in 1927. After his death, his father, Senior Headman Shakopa, honoured his will to the last word. My aunt wished to comply with her late husband's instructions, for she feared that, had she refused to be inherited by me, the spirit of my late uncle would return to haunt her and cause her death. In order to set her free, a ceremony was held during which I gave her official permission to go back to her people and marry a man of her choice. My aunt is still alive at the time of writing and is still grateful to me: she regards my 'concession' as a blessing which has enabled her to have a long life and to escape my late uncle's wrath.

During the two years prior to his death, my uncle attended school with me in the Banamwaze outschool. Our teacher was Jeremiah Lukendo, who was employed by the Methodist mission in Kasenga, near Namwala.[1] In those days, there were no age restrictions for school attendance, which was one of the virtues of missionary education. By the time he died, my uncle was able to read the Ila New Testament. Thereafter, I passed under the care of the leader of Luubwe, Chief Shaloba (Chabang'amba), the husband of my mother's eldest sister, Mwaampu Shakopa. Shaloba's village, Luubwe, lay at a distance of 32 kilometres to the west of the Namwala boma. There, I entered a second outschool. Manned by Silas Kabali, the outschool fell under the

---

[1] Kasenga had been founded in 1909 by the celebrated missionary and anthropologist Rev. Edwin W. Smith. Until 1932, the Methodist Missionary Society was divided into the Primitive Methodist Missionary Society, by which Kasenga and the other missions in Bwila and surrounding areas were staffed, and the Wesleyan Methodist Missionary Society.

almost exclusively on the author's visit to Barotseland in 1958). This, I assume, serves to blot out the frequent conflicts between Congress militants and African MLCs in the mid-1950s. Certainly, in contrast to what Nabulyato implies, a good number of the former did not regard the latter as 'radicals' (p. 51). Reading Nabulyato's monochromatic account, one would hardly guess, for instance, that to the mind of a young Nephas Tembo, 'the whole lot of African MLCs [had] no progressive ideas except yes bwana mentality. [...]. They are after money and a big name.'[5] And two years later, Nkumbula was still of the opinion that 'the depth of [*the African MLCs'*] understanding of what [*was*] going on in the house [*was*] very shallow.'[6]

A similar homogenizing logic can be presumed to have dictated the author's decision not to dwell on his electoral fiasco of 1959. Nabulyato's choice, I maintain, was less the result of conceit (though the defeat against his longstanding rival and fellow Ila, Nkumbula, must have been hard to stomach for Robinson) than the consequence of the author's desire to strengthen his claim of having joined Kaunda's Zambia African National Congress (ZANC) from the moment the party split from the ANC in October 1958. ZANC, it must be remembered, had opted for boycotting the impending elections on account of the exclusionary electoral franchise under which they were to be held; it had been largely because of this resolve that the party had been banned and its top leaders 'rusticated' to remote rural areas by Governor Benson in March 1959. Since ZANC – and its offshoot, UNIP – came to be seen as embodying the most progressive and militant version of Zambian nationalism, by questionably portraying himself as an early supporter of the party, Nabulyato claimed for himself a rightful place within the victorious strand of a nationalist bloc that was nonetheless far more

---

[5] N. Tembo to S. Zukas, Kitwe, 9 June 1954, NAZ, Lusaka, HM 75/PP/1/54/13. Tembo's outburst had been prompted by what he considered to be the African MLCs' weak opposition to an 'anti-picketing bill' (The Penal Code [Amendment] Bill, 1954) passed by the Legislative Council in 1954. For the debate that followed the Bill's second reading, see *Official Verbatim Report of the Debates of the First Session of the Tenth Legislative Council, 10th April – 1st May 1954* (Lusaka, 1954), cols. 238-272.

[6] [H.M. Nkumbula] to T. Fox-Pitt, n.p. [but Lusaka?], 27 September 1956, United National Independence Party's Archives, Lusaka, ANC 5/9. But for a more positive assessment of the African MLCs' role – one occasioned by their 'wonderful' defence of Congress in July of the same year – see *Congress Circular*, 31 July 1956.

complicated and multidimensional than Nabulyato himself is prepared to admit.

The last autobiographical chapter (9) and the following five analytical chapters focus especially on Nabulyato's tenure of the Zambian National Assembly's Speakership and his reflections on the performance of parliamentary government in post-colonial Africa. In my reading, the principal historical value of these sections of the book (written, it should be borne in mind, before the short-lived wave of optimism brought about by tropical Africa's democratisation movements) lies in the unique – if only half-developed – insights they provide into the economic and political crisis that accompanied the twilight of UNIP rule, when, after several years of faithful service, even Nabulyato began to nurture some doubts about Kaunda's statesmanship and the wisdom of continuing with the one-party state experiment.

Speaker Nabulyato was always a strong defender of the prerogatives and independence of Parliament. His stance acquired a manifest political significance in the 1980s, when the Zambian one-party Parliament often served as an outlet for the voicing of widespread concerns about the increasing unpopularity and isolation of the real seats of power in the country: the Executive, the Central Committee of UNIP and, of course, the Presidency. In the closing years of the Second Republic, the most outspoken and foresighted UNIP MPs in the National Assembly and Speaker Nabulyato himself came to be viewed by many as fulfilling the functions of an 'unofficial opposition'. Nabulyato's opaque writing style, full of innuendos, oblique references and seemingly contradictory statements, was the product of a time of great uncertainty and is, in itself, an apt illustration of the pressures that the regime could bring to bear on even some of its most powerful and well-established followers. On more than one occasion, one has the distinctive impression that, his open professions of loyalty to UNIP notwithstanding, Nabulyato speaks of Africa and the inadequacies of its leaders for Zambia to hear. And this impression, of course, is greatly reinforced by the more explicit admissions made in the original documents (i.e. not destined for publication) reproduced in boxes 9 and 12.

When writing about economic polices, a subject on which debate was, if not encouraged, at least tolerated, Nabulyato could afford to be more upfront. By openly defending the principle of free enterprise and the right of individuals to aspire to self-enrichment (chapters 12 and 13), or by pointing out that, far from removing inequality, nationalized economies had merely served to consolidate 'the position of privileged minorities who enjoy plenty in the midst of mass deprivation' (p. 105), Nabulyato was clearly throwing his weight behind the arguments and agenda of a business community whose interests the party in power was proving less and less able to accommodate. Thus, being closely intertwined with the circumstances and context of its compilation, Nabulyato's account offers an informed, insider view of the crisis of an autocratic regime that far too many Zambians have today wrapped in a nostalgic cloud shorn of its multiple failures and deodorized of its most repugnant authoritarian characters.[7]

***

I have said some hard things about Robinson Nabulyato in this introduction. I therefore wish to conclude these brief notes by expressing my most sincere thanks to Mr. Godfrey Nabulyato. Not only did he commission and sponsor the publication of this book, but also, and much more importantly, never sought to hamper my editorial freedom or turn this volume into a glib panegyric. Zambian contemporary memorialists and – may I say it? – political leaders have much to learn from such an honest and self-critical approach to the past.

    Giacomo Macola
    Lusaka
    June 2007

---

[7] For a useful definition of autocracy, with special reference to Zambia, see B.J. Phiri, 'Colonial Legacy and the Role of Society in the Creation and Demise of Autocracy in Zambia, 1964-1991', *Nordic Journal of African Studies*, X, 2 (2001), 224-244, esp. 225.

AUTHOR'S PREFACE

I have been pressed by several friends and others to write an account of my experiences as Speaker of the Zambian National Assembly and my observations of political, economic, historical and social changes in Zambia and the world as a whole. In response, I write with no literary pretensions, but with an honest desire to faithfully describe events as I have witnessed them. The decision about what to include and what to omit has been a difficult one, as I have had to keep within reasonable limits the mass of information available to me.

I am immensely indebted to my wife, Marian, for her patience, endurance and forbearance throughout all the years of my public life. I am also deeply grateful to Mr. Ng'oma Mwelwa Chibesakunda, Clerk of the National Assembly, for reading this manuscript and making invaluable corrections. My Secretary, Mrs. Anne Mwila Kasonde, typed and retyped the manuscript with great patience. Both the Clerk of the National Assembly and my Secretary have always given me close assistance and unfailing support. Words fail me to express my gratitude.

I am also conscious of what I owe to all those who have been members of Parliament during my term of office as Speaker from November 1968. Zambians are wonderful people. Even when debating hotly in the House, they always obeyed my orders to calm down. This made my work bearable. All of the National Assembly's members of staff have also played an important role in jettisoning the heavy burden of my work. All in all, it could not have been any better.

UNIP-centred narrative of national growth in which they were schooled and which still forms the stuff of popular historical discourse in the country. To put it clearly: Nabulyato's homogenizing perspective on the past and understandable desire to emphasize the unity of Northern Rhodesian Africans in their battle against the evils of colonialism mean the volume throws very little light on the many internal lines of conflict and contestation that complicated the landscape of Zambian nationalism from the late 1950s, if not before. In this regard, Nabulyato's account, not unlike those of most other contemporary Zambian political memorialists,[3] replicates the failings of post-Independence political science, whose almost exclusive focus on UNIP and the structures of its developmentalist state provided the unwitting excuse for overlooking or silencing the histories of all the actors and social forces situated outside the ambit of the 'people's party'. A good example of this historical paramnesia – and one that *African Realities* brings to the fore with particular clarity – is the facile dismissal of the unspectacular, but nonetheless significant, challenge to UNIP posed by Nkumbula's ANC throughout the First Republic. The editor's hope is that the publication of *African Realities* might prompt representatives of different political traditions and nationalist projects to put forward their own, alternative accounts of the country's recent past. After all, as John Lonsdale puts it, nationalism has always been 'the work of many wills, with many visions of the future. It is an impoverished nationhood that fails to recognize them.'[4]

It is within the above-sketched intellectual context that some of the volume's *specific* omissions and silences become intelligible. A good case in point is the paucity of information on Nabulyato's work in the LegCo between 1954 and 1958 (though entitled 'Africans in the Legislative Council of Northern Rhodesia', chapter 7 of *African Realities* focuses

---

[3] See E. Mudenda, *Zambia: A Generation of Struggle* (Harare, 1999); A. Sardanis, *Africa: Another Side of the Coin. Northern Rhodesia's Final Years and Zambia's Nationhood* (London and New York, 2002); S.B. Zukas, *Into Exile and Back* (Lusaka, 2002); and J. Mwanakatwe, *Teacher, Politician, Lawyer: My Autobiography* (Lusaka, 2003); A.G. Zulu, *Memoirs of Alexander Grey Zulu* (Lusaka, 2007)

[4] 'Introduction', in E.S. Atieno Odhiambo and J. Lonsdale (eds.), *Mau Mau and Nationhood: Arms, Authority and Narration* (Oxford, Nairobi and Athens [OH], 2003), 5. For a more elaborate treatment of the themes of the above paragraph see J.-B. Gewald, M. Hinfelaar and G. Macola, 'Introduction', in id. (eds.), *One Zambia, Many Histories: Towards a History of Post-Colonial Zambia* (Leiden, forthcoming).

concluding seven chapters. It is felt that this editorial intervention, however radical it might seem, has not altered significantly the substance of Nabulyato's thought. Rather, by eliminating numerous repetitions and some obsolete and/or obscure passages, it has rendered it more concise and readable.

While making formal and stylistic alterations throughout, I have constantly sought, sometimes at the expense of grammatical impeccability and political correctness, to preserve the flavour of Nabulyato's prose. The ideal of 'semiotic faithfulness', however, has not prevented me from adding such significant dates as the author had failed to provide in his original version and changing all the extant dates that could be shown to be wrong. All the explanatory footnotes in the text are my own. So are the documentary boxes, whose main *raison d' être* is to give the reader a general sense of the richness of the archival collection of the NAZ and especially, of course, of the Nabulyato papers, whence the bulk of this book's documentary infrastructure originates.[2] Some of the records reproduced herein serve also to illustrate the natural (and yet so significant for historians) difference in both tone and perspective between 'live' commentaries (i.e. commentaries on still unfolding events) and such later rationalizations as are expressed in an autobiography written several years after the events in question had been consigned to the realm of personal memory and therefore stripped of their most immediately political and polemical purposes.

While providing some important insights into Ila life in the first decades of the twentieth century, the autobiographical chapters of *African Realities* centre principally on the author's political experiences between the late 1940s and the late 1960s. The editor, a professional historian (and the biographer of Harry Nkumbula, one of Nabulyato's most notorious *bêtes noires*!), is naturally inclined to stress the value of these chapters as sources of evidence for the study of the Northern Rhodesian and Zambian past. Mature Zambian readers, on the other hand, might well be attracted to the volume for different reasons – not least, perhaps, the fact that it tends to buttress the simplistic, linear and

---

[2] For a brief presentation of the Nabulyato papers at the NAZ, see M. Hinfelaar and G. Macola, *A First Guide to Non-Governmental Archives in Zambia* (Lusaka, 2004).

CHAPTER 1
Early Life

I was born on 28 October 1916 at Banamwaze village, in the Namwala district of the Southern Province of present-day Zambia (then the British colony of Northern Rhodesia). I am the first born of my mother Nanja (daughter of Senior Headman Shakopa) and my father Shintongo Nabulyato (son of Senior Headman Mwanakwale, shortened to Mwaakwe). My parents were married in 1913, one year before the outbreak of the First World War. Both of my parents were illiterate, but my date of birth was noted down by a European District Officer who had come from the Namwala boma to Banamwaze to recruit soldiers. My birth also coincided with the death of Chief Mukobela (Shekandi) of Baambwe, one of the largest Ila communities in Namwala.

After I was born, my father was recruited into the British Military Forces, first, as a carrier, and, later, as a soldier. I therefore spent my early childhood with my matrilineal uncle Shikalimbwe Shakopa, my mother's elder brother. In those days, the main concern of young Ila boys was to look after cattle. I was no exception to it. My uncle was an enterprising man. He was the first in his area to use a plough pulled by 4 oxen. He was able to do this thanks to the help of two of his Lozi friends, Mubita and Katumwe, who had settled in Shakopa's village after travelling to South Africa and learning the art of taming oxen while working on European farms near Johannesburg. When the oxen had been tamed and a plough purchased, my uncle was so happy that he composed a song in Chiila in praise of his two friends. One of my uncle's oxen was named 'Maachi', after the name of his matrilineal grandfather. The English translation of my uncle's song reads as follows:

> Katumwe bring yokes
> Inspan Maachi, the beautiful ox
> Mubita bring yokes
> Inspan Maachi, the beautiful ox

In the late 1910s, my uncle's deed was rare, though today, in 1988, the plough is commonly used throughout the Southern Province.

Eventually, my uncle's health started to deteriorate. When he realised he was about to die, and since he had no other son, he made me the heir of all of his property. I was even to inherit my uncle's wife, an aunt! That was ridiculous. My uncle Shikalimbwe Shakopa died in 1927. After his death, his father, Senior Headman Shakopa, honoured his will to the last word. My aunt wished to comply with her late husband's instructions, for she feared that, had she refused to be inherited by me, the spirit of my late uncle would return to haunt her and cause her death. In order to set her free, a ceremony was held during which I gave her official permission to go back to her people and marry a man of her choice. My aunt is still alive at the time of writing and is still grateful to me: she regards my 'concession' as a blessing which has enabled her to have a long life and to escape my late uncle's wrath.

During the two years prior to his death, my uncle attended school with me in the Banamwaze outschool. Our teacher was Jeremiah Lukendo, who was employed by the Methodist mission in Kasenga, near Namwala.[1] In those days, there were no age restrictions for school attendance, which was one of the virtues of missionary education. By the time he died, my uncle was able to read the Ila New Testament. Thereafter, I passed under the care of the leader of Luubwe, Chief Shaloba (Chabang'amba), the husband of my mother's eldest sister, Mwaampu Shakopa. Shaloba's village, Luubwe, lay at a distance of 32 kilometres to the west of the Namwala boma. There, I entered a second outschool. Manned by Silas Kabali, the outschool fell under the

---

[1] Kasenga had been founded in 1909 by the celebrated missionary and anthropologist Rev. Edwin W. Smith. Until 1932, the Methodist Missionary Society was divided into the Primitive Methodist Missionary Society, by which Kasenga and the other missions in Bwila and surrounding areas were staffed, and the Wesleyan Methodist Missionary Society.

supervision of Nanzhila Methodist mission.[2] Chief Shaloba had no sons, so I quickly became his favourite adopted son.

Chief Shaloba was fond of making long journeys on foot out of the Namwala district. Since he often took me with him, I began to travel and get to know the world at an early age. In 1929, I accompanied him to Barotseland (present-day Western Province of Zambia). The journey, by foot, took us one month. The trip to the Lozi court was an eye-opener to me. I saw Paramount Chief Yeta III at a distance while my uncle held daily meetings with him.

My second journey with Chief Shaloba took us to Livingstone, then the colony's capital.[3] En route, we passed through Kalomo, whose District Commissioner (DC) was an old Namwala hand, having spent as many as sixteen years among the Ila. His name was Mr. Heath, 'Mwenzhalubilo' to his Ila charges. DC Heath spoke Chiila better than I did! He had been only the second DC in Namwala after Andrew Dale ('Mapani'), the founder of the boma between 1902 and 1905.[4] My uncle and I spent a whole week in Kalomo as guests of Mr. Heath. It was in Kalomo that I was afforded the opportunity of my first ever ride in a car, when our host took us to the railway station to board a train to Livingstone. The train journey was yet another new experience for me. On arrival in Livingstone we were received by the local DC and accommodated at the Police Camp. While there, we were summoned twice to meet the Sir James Maxwell, then the Governor of Northern Rhodesia. Little did I know at the time that, later in life, I would face and fight against the Governor's friends for the Independence of Zambia. After a spell in Livingstone, Chief Shaloba crossed the border into Southern Rhodesia to visit some of his subjects who were working in the coal mines of Wankie. The rest of his entourage (six men and myself)

---

[2] Nanzhila (also spelled Nanzela) had been inaugurated in 1895 among the 'Balumbu' of Sezungo, who was 'probably the descendant of a Lozi refugee who had wrested his territory from the Ila in ca. 1850.' R.J. Fielder, 'Social Change among the Ila-Speaking Peoples of Northern Rhodesia with Particular Reference to Their Relations with the Primitive Methodist Mission', MA thesis, University of Manchester, 1965, 59

[3] It was only in 1935 that the capital of Northern Rhodesia was transferred to Lusaka.

[4] In fact, Native Commissioner and Assistant Magistrate L.C. Heath had only arrived in the district in 1919, the same year in which Dale, who had retired from the British South Africa Company's administration in 1910, died of blackwater fever. Namwala District Notebook, vol. I, National Archives of Zambia (NAZ), Lusaka, KSF 2/1

remained in Livingstone until he came back. As luck would have it, when it was time for us to go back, the Governor was also scheduled to visit Namwala. So we were given a lift on the food-carrying lorry of the Governor all the way from Livingstone to Namwala. For me, a small boy, that was a wonderful experience indeed.

In May 1932, when Chief Shezongo (Ngulwa) of Luchena died, Chief Shaloba took me with him to the funeral. I then had a chance to see Nanzhila mission, which was only two kilometres away from the village where the funeral was being held. Each morning I would walk to the mission to watch the school pupils lining up to go into their classrooms. How I wanted to be like them! In August of the same year, Rev. Ernest Stamp, the missionary in charge of Nanzhila, and his wife, Muriel Clare, came to Luubwe to examine the pupils of the outschool I had been attending. I did so well in the tests that they decided to take me back with them to Nanzhila mission's boarding school for further education. Thus began my two-year-long stay at Nanzhila, where I paid 7/- 6d. per year as school fees.[5] In 1934, when Rev. Stamp and his wife went to England on furlough, they decided to send me to the Kafue Training Institute, for they feared that, if I had remained at Nanzhila without their supervision, I might have run back to Luubwe and Chief Shaloba, whom I missed greatly.[6]

I am greatly indebted to Rev. Stamp and his wife, who regarded me as their black son since the day they took me under their care in Nanzhila. I have never been happier working under a European than when I briefly served under Rev. Stamp at the Kafue Training Institute. Later on, Rev. Stamp became the General Superintendent of the Methodist Church in Northern Rhodesia and was even appointed to the colony's Legislative Council to represent African interests. While Rev. Stamp died in September 1970, the 93-year-old Muriel is still living in England. I usually go to see her whenever I happen to visit the United Kingdom.

The yearly school fees at Kafue were £3. The money I had earned from Chief Shaloba saw me through the first year. Thereafter, I earned

---

[5] Although the author does not say so, it is very likely that he completed Std. I and II at Nanzhila.
[6] The 'Kafue *Native* Training Institute' changed its name to the 'Kafue Training Institute' in 1936

my school fees by working at the mission during the long school holidays between May and August. In addition to this, students kept a vegetable garden and a chicken run from which we were able to sell vegetables and eggs to Europeans in Kafue railway township. There was a hotel, too, in Kafue. Thus European railway workers provided a ready market for what we produced at the Institute. The distance between the Institute and the town, however, was considerable: eleven kilometres. On the other hand, school equipment, uniforms and blankets were supplied freely by the school once the fees had been paid.

While my mother's village, Shakopa's, where I spent my early childhood, was home to me, I was not nearly as familiar with my father's place. As I said earlier, my father had enlisted in the British Army during the Great War. Since he was absent for a long time and was presumed dead in the war, Senior Headman Shakopa, after being approached by Headman Muyanichila (Shaabwa) of Kabanga, some 23 kilometres from Banamwaze, allowed my mother to remarry. When my father eventually made his way back home, Shakopa sought to get my mother back to my father, but the latter objected. Shakopa then declared himself willing to return the 26 head of cattle that my father had paid to him as bridewealth, but my father refused, arguing that the cattle represented a tangible link between the two families and that, if they were ever to be returned, he would rather they be given to me, his son, once I was old enough. My mother and Headman Muyanichila had one son, Oswell Nzangwa Shaabwa. When her second husband died, my mother did not remarry. Eventually, I took Oswell under my care and made sure he received a good education. When Oswell died in 1978, I was appointed as the sole guardian of his ten children.

Many Baila families owned slaves, most of whom, however, would eventually get assimilated into their owners' families as classificatory relatives. When my paternal grandfather, Senior Headman Mwanakwale, was about to die, he nominated one of his nephews of slave descent to inherit his position. This was an interim measure adopted during my father's adolescence. After my father's return from the front, his classificatory cousin, who regarded himself as a mere regent, was prepared to give up the headmanship and see my father installed in his stead. Initially, my father resisted the offer, but was later convinced to inherit his father's place by the other headmen and by Chief Chilyabufu of Banamwaze. My father, however, did not live long in his new position. When he died, his erstwhile regent was still alive and resolved to have me selected as headman. I, however, picked another relative to look after the village. When both the latter and the old regent died, I selected yet another relative – an adopted son of my father – to act in my stead. When he, too, died in 1987, I finally took on the duties of village headman. Since I was then still serving as Speaker of the National Assembly, I left someone to attend to simple problems, while making sure that all complicated matters affecting village life were referred to me. The foregoing account clarifies that among the Baila, and possibly in Zambia as a whole, slavery was not punitive – so much so that slaves could rise within families and even to chiefly positions. Even today, there are many such positions which have been and are occupied by slave lineages in various parts of Zambia.

Another point that readers will not have failed to grasp from this quick survey of my early years is that going to school in the first decades of the twentieth century was nothing short of an ordeal. Schools – mainly mission ones – were few and far between. To attend them often meant travelling over long and dangerous distances. The lack of means of transport other than travelling on foot is one of the reasons why female education has lagged far behind in the country. For example, two whole days were necessary to reach Nanzhila mission from Luubwe village. The distance between Namwala and Monze, where we usually boarded the train to Kafue, could only be covered in a week or so of arduous walking. During the trek, we would sleep in the bush, for villages were also scattered far and wide. By the 1940s, however, transport had become more readily available in Northern Rhodesia, thus enabling a few girls (among them my wife, Marian) to reach such good schools as Chipembi mission school in what is today Kabwe district. Owing to the dearth of female education in Northern Rhodesia, some of our returning labour migrants came back home with Southern

Rhodesian or South African wives, who were generally better educated than our women could be. At the time of writing, the trend has changed, for our Zambian women are now as presentable as any other women – educated, beautiful or clean, and civilised.

CHAPTER 2

My School Days and Teaching Career

The Kafue Institute, which I entered in 1935, was a training institution for such various trades as Carpentry, Blacksmithing, Building, Bookkeeping and Typing. It also offered courses in Teacher Training, Evangelist Training and courses in Crop Management, Animal Husbandry, etc. Sewing and Cookery courses were normally taken up by the wives of adult male trainees. The Institute had been founded in 1918 by Rev. J.R. Fell thanks to the donation of a British benefactor, Mr. Clixby. Thus the area covered by the school became known as the Clixby Estate. The Institute was located eight kilometres to the west of the Road Bridge on the Kafue River; students used to get caught by crocodiles as they went to draw water, swim or fish in the river. At the Institute I completed Std. VI – then the highest academic achievement open to Northern Rhodesian Africans – and learnt Carpentry, Evangelism, Crop and Animal Husbandry, Teacher Training and Health Care. I also joined the Pathfinders. Started by Rev. J.F. Bedford, the Pathfinders would later evolve into the Scout Movement of Northern Rhodesia.

In 1937, having completed my course of study at Kafue, I went back to Nanzhila as a teacher or 'district agent'. I was then 21. At Nanzhila, I worked with Rev. L.W.S. Price. Rev. Price, a Zambian, had by then acquired two volumes by Marcus Garvey, a Jamaican.[1] These were prohibited publications in the then Northern Rhodesia. Rev. Price lent them to me. I went into the bush on a Saturday afternoon, slept there and completed reading both volumes by Sunday morning. After making

---

[1] Rev. Leonard Shapela Price, a 'half-cast' child, had been brought up and then adopted by Rev. John W. Price, Edwin Smith's successor at Kasenga mission. The writings of Garvey to which young Nabulyato had access must have been A.J. Garvey (ed. and compiler), *Philosophy and Opinions of Marcus Garvey* (New York, 1923) and *Philosophy and Opinions of Marcus Garvey or Africa for the Africans* (New York, 1926)

> **Box 1: Nabulyato on Marcus Garvey**
>
> Garvey's influence on Nabulyato was clearly very significant, as attested by the references to the Jamaican writer and campaigner in the Personal Notebook that Nabulyato compiled in the 1940s. In a passage entitled 'Bravery', young Robinson wrote:
>
> *'No trace of cowardice has been found in Marcus Garvey, even by his bitterest foes for he was courageous. His dream of "Africa for the Africans" shall surely come to its climax. All Europeans have no room in Africa for exploitation as we, Africans, have no room in their countries for anything. Cowardice and fear allowed us to be taken possession of [by] the whites for a long time [...]. It is no use being afraid of these European nations. They are human beings like us. We have blood, feelings, passions and ambitions just as they have. Why therefore should we allow them to trample down our rights and deprive us of our liberty [?]'*
>
> (Source: R.M. Nabulyato, Personal Notebook, [1940s], National Archives of Zambia (NAZ), Lusaka, HM 79/PP/10/1)

notes from the two volumes, I returned them to Rev. Price, who then sent them back to the man who had given them to him. I later learnt the latter was none other than Isaac Clements Muwamba, a Malawian who worked as a Senior Boma Clerk in Namwala and a very close friend to both of us.[2] This is where doubts about British rule in the then Northern Rhodesia grasped me.

The difficulties I encountered in working with some missionaries were also significant in shaping my outlook. Most white mission workers from 1900 to about 1930 did not have high education but were endowed with the willingness to serve the Spirit of God and did good missionary work. Kafue Training Institute changed its educational profile when men like Rev. L. Morley BA, BD, Rev. J.F. Bedford BA, and

---

[2] Isaac Clements was the brother of the more famous Ernest Muwamba, the founder of an African welfare association in Ndola in 1930. R.I. Rotberg, *The Rise of Nationalism in Central Africa: The Making of Malawi and Zambia, 1873-1964* (Cambridge [Mass.], 1965), 127, n. 27.

Rev. C.R. Hopgood BA, BD, became involved in its running. These were our teachers when we were students. It was a real pleasure to be instructed by these efficient teachers. After I became a teacher, I continued to enjoy working with men like Revs. Bedford and Hopgood. Even some of these 'intellectuals', however, were affected by the racial prejudices typical of the time.

Between 1942 and 1944, I attended the Jeanes Teachers Training School with a view to obtaining the H.T.C. or Higher Teacher's Certificate, the equivalent of Std. 8 or Form II. Inaugurated in 1929 in Mazabuka by the founder of the Kafue Institute, Rev. J.R. Fell, the Jeanes School was by then located in Chalimbana, to the east of Lusaka, and

---

Box 2: Chalimbana, 1942-1944

Nabulyato's contemporary assessment of Mrs. Robertson and, more in general, his experiences in Chalimbana was distinctly harsher than in his later autobiography. In his Personal Notebook, under the title 'At Chalimbana Govt. School', we read:

'There I suffered under prejudices thro' the employment of my fellow Africans who undermined me. The Principal's wife – a hag – used to swagger, look and talk down upon students who were ex-teachers of some years' service. She pretended to like Africans in their presence. But in their absence she said "the smell of an African is like that of a female crocodile". At that school we were due 4 uniforms from 1942-1944, we signed forms, but received 3. On inquiring into the matter, it was turned round into an insolence on the Principal concerned. The way we were made to apologize, yet right, was wonderfully puzzling and at the same time did not get the 4th uniform. I myself was unreasonable suspected and nominated to have been one of the chief "Ring Leaders". The Principal's wife kept an eye on my life more than anything else [...]. All what I gathered at Chalimbana was that "Africans are being trained to realise and acknowledge the British power and thus be a better tool for the pilfering European."'

(Source: R.M. Nabulyato, Personal Notebook, [1940s], NAZ, HM 79/PP/10/1)

placed under the care of Rev. David Maxwell Robertson, formerly of Lubwa mission in the Northern Province. While at Chalimbana, I one day felt insulted by the Principal's wife, Mrs Robertson MA, our Biology teacher. She derogatorily called us 'Boys'; and yet we were adult teachers in service training! I protested, pointing out that even though she was our teacher, she had no right to refer to us as 'boys', not least because she was a woman fit for any of us to marry. Oh, she screamed and ran out of the classroom to report to her husband! I was then saved from expulsion by Safeli Chileshe, a senior teacher who was also in charge of the adult students. But my little rebellion served its purpose, for Mrs. Robertson soon learnt to be respectful to all of us. Rather less problematical was my relationship with Stanley Vivian BA, who taught us Psychology, English, Mathematics and Economics. Mr. Vivian was an excellent teacher, clear, concise and to the point. He was later transferred to Nyasaland (colonial Malawi), where he became the Principal of the local Jeanes School.

In the mid-1940s, when I returned to the Kafue Training Institute as headmaster, I had to deal with a Principal who did not understand the system of education in Northern Rhodesia.[3] One day, he brought return forms from the headquarters of the Department of African Education in Mazabuka. Although these were meant to be filled in by the Principals of the various schools, he requested me to assist him in a commandeering way. I refused to cooperate and told him that the compilation of the forms in question was the prerogative of Principals. I could not do the job for him while he was paid an allowance for it. Poor man! He shouted at me and said, 'as a Britisher you must respect me, we rule this country and you cannot disobey my orders or I speak to you in your place of ...' He did not complete his sentence. I repeatedly asked what he meant by 'my place'. None of us ever forgot this hard exchange of words. For the missionary, it turned out to be a blessing in disguise: when he went back to England on furlough, he resolved to return to college to acquire an Education Diploma. As for me, his incomplete sentence kept nagging me. I thought he wanted to say that 'my place' was that of a serf, a slave, a dog, a monkey, a black native or 'boy', as

---

[3] The Principal, whose name Nabulyato kindly omits to mention, was Rev. J.L. Matthews.

Africans of all ages were then referred to by whites. However, black women did receive respect from white men, especially in their bedrooms at night! It was primarily the attitude of my white co-workers that led to my resignation from teaching late in 1949.

Another factor that militated against my continuing stay in Kafue were the difficulties I began to experience in receiving my mail after I had become the first Secretary-General of the Northern Rhodesia African Congress in 1948. The night before my departure from Kafue, all the students organised a concert in my honour and presented me with a costly gift: a 'Swan' fountain pen. My pupils understood my motives and supported my decision to resign. During the farewell concert, I thanked them and promised that this 'gift of the pen from you all is a spear I will "swan" with to hunt until food and relish will be provided for us all in this country.' They all understood I was forecasting independence for the Africans of Northern Rhodesia. Among my students at Kafue were Sikota Wina, Andrew Mutemba, Nephas Tembo, Justin Chimba and Jonathan Chivunga – to mention but a few of those who would later occupy prominent position in the government of independent Zambia.

> **Box 3: Nabulyato on the Missionaries**
>
> Nabulyato's relationships with his Methodist employers deteriorated to such an extent that, in an entry in his Personal Notebook entitled 'Africa and the Missionaries', he offered the following, damning critique. Borrowing freely from George Padmore's *How Britain Rules Africa* (London, 1936), 391, he described the missionaries as:
>
> *'[T]he disguised agents of Imperialism. Therefore all sufferings inflicted on the Africans by the Imperial Govt. are a direct result of the Missionaries' collusion for the exploitation of Africa. Therefore Africans must realise that they are paid low salaries either by Missionary Societies, Govt. or the Company, because the Europeans want Africans to be poor and dependent. [...]. When missionaries come to*

> *Africa, their preached aim is to "save the African from paganism". But when they reach Africa, they tend to be hunting for faults among their Christians and thus black-list (teachers as well) some intelligent and good men from any kind of employment in the country – which punishment is more than cruelty as it means hunger, starvation, nakedness, poverty etc. on the person concerned. Therefore as missionaries come out to save Africa from paganism – as they say – [they] should not be dismayed [by] the sins they meet. They should try to prevent the commission of sins rather than punish cruelly and probably ruin a person's career in life. Religion is just a way of thinking and believing and should not be a burden to the lives of men. Jesus Christ taught and reserved [sic] Peter in spite of all Peter's wickedness. In the long run Peter became the stone or Foundation of the "church of Christ". The missionaries collect financial charities and grants from people and Govt. and yet the salaries of the Mission Servants do not rise or improve. [...]. So the missionaries betray us to Govt. and thus misrepresent us to the Govt. When they come to the Africans they turn round and misrepresent the Govt. to the Africans. Therefore they are cheats and liars.'*
>
> (Source: R.M. Nabulyato, Personal Notebook, [1940s], NAZ, HM 79/PP/10/1)

Having brought my association with Kafue to an end, I returned to Banamwaze, where I used my savings to open a small village shop, the Banamwaze Store. I invested £25 in the store. The licence fee cost me 2 shillings and 6 pence. My young brother Oswell Shaabwa and I settled down to work. I also began to buy and breed cattle so as to use oxen for ploughing. This was the art I had learnt from my late uncle Shikalimbwe Shakopa and refined through the Kafue courses in Crop and Animal Husbandry. Since I could also rotate crops, villagers learnt from what I was doing and began to copy my farming methods. When I settled in Banamwaze at the end of 1949, people could still be found starving in the midst of plenty. Today, people in Banamwaze only starve when there is a drought or when floods and locusts damage their crops. I am happy to have given some exemplary service to the area. When I relocated in Banamwaze, my ambition was to face the realities of life with the local people, but, as we shall see in later chapters, politics would soon disrupt my plans.

I made another contribution to Bamwaze in 1951, when I organised people to make and burn bricks for a school, teachers' houses and three dormitories for children from distant villages. I also impressed upon the people the need for small financial contributions to pay the builders and other workers. Upon being informed of the initiative, the Northern Rhodesian government supplied the school with door and window frames, doors, cement and corrugated iron sheets. This effort resulted in Banamwaze being provided for the first time with a decent school. (The school, I am afraid, is now falling to pieces owing to lack of maintenance. The people are tired of constant appeals to self-help because they feel government does not help.) Marian, my future wife, was the daughter of the Banamwaze school teacher, Joshua Muwana. Marian always returned to Banamwaze when her school, Chipembi Girls, closed for holidays. Marian and I got married in 1950. We have a daughter and five sons.

CHAPTER 3
The Roots of my Political Career

While teaching at Kafue in the 1940s, I subscribed to many of the newspapers circulating in the then Northern Rhodesia, Southern Rhodesia and Nyasaland. While the *Bantu Mirror* and the *African Weekly* were published in Salisbury (present-day Harare), I also subscribed to two of the Northern Rhodesian papers: the *Central African Post*, the owner of which was Dr. Alexander Scott, and *Mutende*, the government newspaper for Africans. Thus I kept myself fully informed about events in the region and the world at large. I also read many types of books. One which I remember vividly was *How Britain Rules Africa*, by George Padmore,[1] whom I would later meet in London in 1952. Alongside the works of Padmore and the aforementioned Garvey, I was also familiar with Dr. Aggrey's writings and was particularly touched by his metaphor to the effect that to make a harmonious music on a piano or organ, one had to play both 'white and black notes'.[2]

But my political formation also owed much to Hedley J. Roberts BA, who worked with us at Kafue as a schoolmaster. (Roberts would later resign from the Methodist Church and become the principal of Munali Secondary School, the only full-blown secondary school in Northern Rhodesia built by the colonial government.) Roberts was a very useful and open-minded gentleman. I will always remember his remarks during one of our historical discussions. My Std. VI students were then learning about Australia and the extermination of its aboriginal population by white settlers. Roberts argued that this kind of thing

---
[1] The original reads: '*British Rule in Africa*'.
[2] The piano keyboard was the symbol that the famous educationalist, James E.K. Aggrey, chose for the shield of the Prince of Wales College at Achimota, near Accra, Ghana, after being appointed Vice-Principal in 1922; http://www.bartleby.com/65/ag/Aggrey-J.html (accessed on 11 June 2007).

would never occur in Northern Rhodesia or Africa as a whole, because, while the aborigines of Australia or the Red Indians of North America or the Maoris of New Zealand were few in number and could be easily annihilated, the black people of Northern Rhodesia and Africa were millions. He went on to say that, no matter what the plans of the local white settlers were, sooner or later, the government of Northern Rhodesia would be in the hand of the country's black majority. What a brave thing for a white man to say! How courageous of him to challenge widespread prejudices against the black man in Northern Rhodesia and Africa as a whole! Thanks to his progressiveness, Roberts could visualise the future of Northern Rhodesia and Africa. It is impossible not to respect such views.

By the mid-1940s, the European settlers of the Rhodesias and Nyasaland were busy pressing for self-government or responsible government through the amalgamation of the three countries. The polity they envisaged was to be run along the racist lines of Southern Rhodesia, where Lord Malvern (then Sir Godfrey Huggins) was Prime Minister. The settlers were convinced that Africans were not educated enough to participate in such a civilised form of government. Initially, however, the Colonial Office continued to adhere to its multi-racial principles and did not give in easily to the settlers' plans. Through the newspapers, I was able to follow the increasingly heated debates on amalgamation or closer association and to realize I was not alone in feeling deeply disturbed by them. While I got wind of the political activities of the future president of Malawi, Dr. Hastings Kamuzu Banda, then a medical doctor in London, I also learnt of the mushrooming of welfare associations or societies in Northern Rhodesia. I was particularly encouraged by the activism of Donald Siwale, whose Mwenzo Welfare Association had been founded as early as the 1920s. I would later work hand in hand with Siwale in both the Northern Rhodesia African Congress and the African Representative Council.

Alongside politics, literature and translation work were the other interests I cultivated throughout the 1940s. My first literary venture took place in 1941, while I was still at Nanzhila, when I participated in an

English essay competition sponsored by the African Literature Committee of Northern Rhodesia and advertised in *Mutende*. I chose to write on the following subject: 'It has been said that the Bible and the Bicycle are the two most valuable things that the European has brought to Africa. Discuss this statement'. Both Moses Mubitana, of the Kafue Training Institute, and I won prizes, thus bringing honour to the Methodist Church for the exceptionally high standard of our English.[3] The then General Superintendent of the Methodist Church, Rev. J.G. Soulsby, did not just send us letters of congratulations, but he even made trips from his headquarters in Lusaka to Kafue and Nazhila to give us personal encouragement.

From that time onwards, Mr. Mubitana and I were given all sorts of Church literary work. Mubitana was entrusted with the task of translating Bunyan's famous *Pilgrim's Progress* into Chiila, [4]while I worked on a translation of *God's Family in the World* with Rev. Matthew S. Lucheya and Rev. C.R. Hopgood.[5] Still in the 1940s, Enock Kaavu, a brilliant scholar, embarked on a novel in English entitled *Namusiya at the Mines*. Unfortunately, he died before he could finish it. I was then requested to complete it in English and to produce a Chiila version, too.[15] As I write, the book is out of print, despite many people, including some members of the University of Zambia, having tried to get me to issue a new edition. My collaboration with Rev. Hopgood also resulted in the translation of portions of the Bible into Chiila and Chitonga for the Methodist Church. We concentrated on the Old Testament, since a Chiila version of the New Testament had already been produced by Rev. Dr. E.W. Smith. When the latter learnt of my and Hopgood's work at

---

[3] In the original typescript, Nabulyato gave the following as the title of his prize-wining essay: 'Means of communications by 1980 in Northern Rhodesia'. The correct title is to be found in *Mutende*, 9 October 1941. While Nabulyato won the third prize for its essay, Mubitana won the second for a piece on the subject of 'Beer: its use and misuse'. The only Methodist teacher to win a first prize was Harry Nkumbula, the then headmaster of the Mufulira African School, who wrote a 'Brief tribal history of the Baila'. *Mutende*, 23 April 1942.

[4] Mubitana's translation was published in 1942 by the Lutterworth Press.

[5] The full title of the book, by G.A. Gollock and T.C. Young, was *God's Family in the World: Sixteen Bible Studies for African Christians with Suggestions for Talking Meetings* (London, 1936). It is not clear whether Nabulyato, Lucheya and Hopgood's Ila or Tonga translation was ever published. Certainly, no book by this title is to be found in the *List of Books Sponsored by the Nyasaland Education Department and by the Northern Rhodesia African Literature Committee and by the Joint Publications Bureau of Northern Rhodesia and Nyasaland* (Lusaka, 1949).

Kafue, he came out of retirement to lend us his assistance. By then, the founder of Kasenga mission was 84 years of age, but still physically fit and mentally alert. Dr. Smith had a deep knowledge of Chiila, having been the first one to reduce it to writing at the beginning of the century. He asked me to prepare a paper with my criticisms of some of his earlier translations. Although the essay was written, Dr. Smith never had the chance to use it, for he died shortly afterwards. It was a great honour and pleasure to have been in contact with such a genius of the Ila language.

I also worked with a Catholic priest and Chibemba expert, Father F. Tanguy of Malole mission in the Northern Province. Fr. Tanguy taught me Chibemba, a knowledge of which was needed for my Matriculation Examinations of South Africa. Since neither Tonga nor Ila were then accepted, I had to select Chibemba as the vernacular language in which to be examined. I can hardly speak Chibemba, but did very well in my *written* examinations! Among the Chibemba books prescribed for my South African examinations was the *Ifya Bukaya* series of Bemba school readers published in the early 1930s by the White Fathers of Chilubula mission. Oh I liked them tremendously!

Box 4: Nabulyato and Colonial Racism

Nabulyato's opposition to racism was both visceral and reasoned, as attested by the following excerpts from his Personal Notebook ('Giving a chance to the Blacks' and 'Africans' natural birthright and the Europeans'):

'If the African is inferior why circumvent him; why suppress his talent or initiative; why rob him of his independent gifts; why fool him out of the rights of his country; why imprison his intelligence and exploit his ignorance; why keep him down by the laws of inequality; why not leave him alone to his own intelligence; why not give him a chance to grow and develop as he sees fit; [...] why not allow him free and unhampered to travel toward nationhood. If the whites are good sportsmen, they will give the blacks a chance, and I predict that in fifty years, undisturbed or unmolested, I will show you a nation of proud, refined and cultured

> black men and women, whose comeliness will outshine that of the age of Solomon."That an African is a "damned nigger" and is predestined to be always a hewer of wood and a carrier of water for the blessed European is a statement worth [sic] objected to by nature. Therefore God who made the African black is not foolish. The European may think a black man is meant by God to be a tool of the wise European, but as far as he is a human being, God knows his part and he should be humanly considered as a person. Therefore it is worthwhile for the European to recognise and value the humanity as revealed in the African by God. [...]. Troubles between African and European do not arise among individuals simply because one is superior than the other, but because one, the European, trumpets too much of his position in comparison with the other.'
>
> (Source: R.M. Nabulyato, Personal Notebook, [1940s], NAZ, Lusaka, HM 79/PP/10/1)

Despite all the praises that the whites bestowed on me for my literary and translation work, I knew I was black and still perhaps regarded as a monkey or an illiterate African on account of the colour of my skin. My growing nationalism thus overpowered all the superficial praises about my mental powers and command of the English language. If I could see as Dr. Aggrey saw, why not struggle to fly to freedom and independence? Why accept false and empty praises? These questions needed practical answers from me.

CHAPTER 4

Joining Forces with Some Other People

In the previous three chapters, I have written about the individual influences that affected me. In this chapter, I will describe the organisations that helped me to join forces with other Africans and non-Africans.

In June 1948, I received an invitation to attend the General Conference or Meeting of the two-year-old Federation of African Societies of Northern Rhodesia (FASNR) which was to be held in Lusaka. I accepted the invitation and travelled to Lusaka from Kafue on a Friday evening so as to be back for work in Kafue by Sunday evening. This organisation was a new umbrella-body for both rural and urban welfare associations in Northern Rhodesia. Welfare associations were usually in the hands of African civil servants, who used them to share views and associate with fellow citizens. At the time, the Executive Committee of the FASNR consisted of Dauti L. Yamba, President; L. Mufana Lipalile, Vice-President; George Kaluwa, Secretary; and John Richmond (an African), Assistant Secretary. There were no other office-bearers as membership of the organization was still free.[1]

At the conference of July 1948, which Yamba did not attend, I was elected General Secretary, while the former Secretary, Kaluwa, became my deputy.[2] Yamba was replaced as President by Godwin Mbikusita-

---

[1] Nabulyato may be mistaken here, for in 1947 a N.S. Liyanda was seemingly serving as the Treasurer of the FASNR. Also, its Assistant Secretary before 1948 was not Richmond (elected to the post in that same year), but Joseph Y. Mumba. See list of office-bearers given in G.W.C. Kaluwa to Director of African Education, Mazabuka, 27 March 1947, encl. in Director of African Education to Secretary for Native Affairs, Mazabuka, 3 April 1947, NAZ, SEC 2/1119, and 'Congress of Northern Rhodesia African Societies', encl. R.M. Nabulyato to Secretary for Native Affairs, 27 August 1948, NAZ, SEC 2/1119.

[2] In fact, Kaluwa was initially elected Deputy Treasurer and only became Vice-Secretary-General in 1951.

Lewanika. During the meeting, we resolved to be more political than before. Expressions of this new militancy were the decision to begin to refer to Northern Rhodesia as 'Zambezia' and to rename our organisation the 'Northern Rhodesia African Congress'. We also resolved to draw up a new constitution. But we had neither money nor any typewriters or printing and duplicating machines. The only places where printing or duplicating could be carried out were either the Government Printer, which we obviously could not use, or Dr. Scott's Astonian Press, which we could not hire. But a friendly Asian with a typewriter and duplicating machine offered us his services free of charge. His name was R.D. Patel of Kanjombe Stores in Cha Cha Cha Road, Lusaka. Patel had come to Northern Rhodesia from India in 1925. He opened his doors to us, being prompted to do so by his admiration for Ghandi's struggles both in South Africa and India, who's Independence the Mahatma had achieved in 1945. While Mr. Patel's shop became a kind of headquarters for all of our work, our real home was at Mr. and Mrs. Anderson Hiwa's house in Mapoloto, Chilenje, a suburb of Lusaka. The Hiwas' home became the hub of African political activity. We took all of our visitors there: Europeans, chiefs and other people who came to confer with us. At the same time, we drew spiritual and moral inspirations from Rev. John Longa Membe of the Methodist Episcopal Church.

In our efforts to draw up a constitution for the new Congress, we were aided by many African teachers both at Munali Secondary School and the Jeanes School. Some of these friends were Hubert Siwale, Safeli Chileshe, Henry Makulu, John Chikungu, Imanga Maliande. Other pillars of our organisation in Lusaka were Mr. Chewemukulu, who worked at the Lusaka boma, Joseph Mwanakatwe, of the High Court, E. Chalungumana, and Edwin Mlongoti and Edward Kateka, both of whom worked for the department of Information and Broadcasting. Other Lusaka-based supporters from outside the civil service were Pascale Sokota, A. Hambayi, of Diamond and Martin Law Firm, Smutts Munkanta of Taxi Firm, Lewis Changufu and two Methodist reverends: Isaac C. Mumpansha and M.S. Lucheya. I have particularly vivid

Box 5: The Northern Rhodesia African Congress

Reproduced below are the principal resolutions adopted by the General Annual Conference of the Federation of Northern Rhodesia African Societies, Lusaka, 9-13 July 1948

'The General Annual Meeting of the Federation of Northern Rhodesia African Societies sat at Lusaka from the 9th to 13th July 1948 as announced in the Press previously, and Delegates from various affiliated Societies including Salisbury and Bulawayo Branches and members of the Public attended the meeting.

The following resolutions were passed at this meeting:

1. A letter to the Right Honourable the Secretary of State for the Colonies, through the Honourable the Secretary for Native Affairs, thanking the British Government for:

a) The appointment of African Delegation to London on Responsible Government.

b) The appointment of two African Members to the Legislative Council.

2. <u>Re-nomination of Sir Stewart Gore-Browne</u>.

The Federation of Northern Rhodesia African Societies is not in a position to support this as the Honourable member has refused to withdraw himself from supporting the Constitutional Proposals, and as he had suggested to resign once Africans refuse to support the proposals, the Federation cannot understand why he would like to be re-nominated. Those other members of the African Representative Council who voted for his re-nomination have misrepresented their constituencies.

3. Northern Rhodesia should be declared a Protectorate in the truest sense of the word and the misleading name "Northern Rhodesia" changed to "QUEEN VICTORIA PROTECTORATE".

4. Africans are as opposed to the Federation of the two Rhodesias and Nyasaland as they are to responsible Government and Amalgamation.

> 5. *A Committee was formed to prepare a Memorandum against Constitutional Proposals for the African Delegation to London.*
>
> 6. *It was unanimously agreed that the Federation of Northern Rhodesia African Societies should change into a CONGRESS and a Committee, under the chairmanship of the General Secretary, was appointed to draft a Constitution suiting a Congress, which will be circulated to affiliated Societies, other African Organisations and certain individuals and published in the Press for comments. Comments are to be communicated to the General-Secretary, c/o Kafue Training Institute, P.O. Kafue, Northern Rhodesia.'*
>
> (Source: 'Congress of Northern Rhodesia African Societies', encl. R.M. Nabulyato to Secretary for Native Affairs, 27 August 1948, NAZ, SEC 2/1119.)

memories of the taxi-driver, Mr. Munkanta, who twice bolted Harry Mwaanga Nkumbula (the President of the Congress from 1951) and myself out of dangerous meetings in Livingstone and the Copperbelt. He saved us from arrest on several occasions; without him, Congress would have flopped in its infancy. He was an asset to the organisation.

Although we were all doing Congress work on a part-time basis (I myself used to travel to Lusaka by bicycle or train every Friday evening and return to Kafue on Sunday) the name 'Congress' frightened the government of Northern Rhodesia. It reminded them of the South African and Indian Congresses, which had stirred up real agitation against their respective colonial governments. However, since many of our best and most educated brains were in the civil service, we had to play it soft. By the time the Munali Secondary School moved to its present site on the Great East Road, John M. Mwanakatwe BA and Joseph B. Mwemba BA had both returned from studies abroad and joined the school's teaching staff. Every evening I would crawl there to consult with the two of them at their residences. What a tremendous help I obtained! However, as time went on, some jealous person reported my nightly visits to the school to the Principal.[3] Fortunately,

---
[3] Clifford Little.

the latter was a liberal white man who understood the African plight. He invited me to a cup of tea one afternoon and informed me that he did not mind my visits to 'relatives and friends' at the school. Well, some black people were just that type; I later had to face many more of that kind who became paid agents and informers against the African Congress. All African sell outs, spies and secret agents on the white government's pay-roll were nicknamed 'Capricorns', from the name of the Capricorn Africa Society, a secret organisation of white settlers who opposed the 'soft' attitude of the British government towards Africans. The aim of their secret organisation was to speed up white domination in Central and Southern Africa. Nationalists regarded African adherents to the Society as traitors or opportunists who were good for nothing on earth.[4] Another crucial decision taken at the conference of 1948 was finally to implement membership and subscription fees to the Congress. Mateyo Kakumbi was elected as the party's Treasurer. It was he who, thanks to a donation of £25 from Sir Stewart Gore-Browne, opened the Congress' first bank account. Thereafter all subscriptions went into this account, and the party became less dependent on individual donations for conducting correspondence and other office work. In the late 1940s we were joined by two other white friends: Commander Thomas Fox-Pitt and Simon Ber Zukas. Fox-Pitt was a former Provincial Commissioner (PC) who had been saved from a marauding lion by an African in the Eastern Province. Since he owed his life to an African, he had become an African at heart. Zukas, an engineer by profession, had his own pro-African views. During the struggle against Federation, he was detained and later deported to Britain, never to return until the attainment of Independence in 1964. These two friends worked very closely with the Northern Rhodesia African Congress. I am happy that, while Commander Fox-Pitt died in England in 1986, Mr. and Mrs. Zukas have settled in Zambia. This shows that black Africans are willing to accommodate good people of all races.

---

[4] Nabulyato's assessment of the Capricorn Africa Society is, of course, historically untenable. Not only was the organization not secret, but its members were also openly liberal and multi-racial. What made the Society anathema to African nationalists, however, was its support for Federation. See B.J. Phiri, 'The Capricorn Africa Society: A Study of Liberal Politics in Northern Rhodesia/Zambia, 1949-1972', PhD thesis, Dalhousie University, 1991.

In virtue of his position as Member of the Legislative Council (MLC) of Northern Rhodesia representing African Interests, Sir Gore-Browne was always close to all African organisations without exception. He attended all African meetings, be they government-sponsored or independent, such as those of the Congress. It was thanks to Gore-Browne that we succeeded in getting the colonial government to commit itself, through the Secretary for Native Affairs (SNA), to a policy statement regarding the relationship between the African civil service and the Congress. The concession was made that 'African civil servants may attend Congress meetings and make statements of fact.'[5] We were happy with this statement, for African civil servants were now free to participate in Congress affairs without putting their careers and livelihoods at risk. To be sure, we were aware that, by opening the Congress to civil servants, we were exposing ourselves to the risk of infiltration by government spies. However, we were confident we would be able to spot these latter under whatever disguise they appeared.

---

[5] The position of the Secretary for Native Affairs was, in fact, slightly more complicated. Writing to Nabulyato in October 1948, he had stated: 'that (a) African Civil Servants may be allowed to join your Congress (b) African Civil Servants should not be permitted to become office-bearers of your Congress (c) African Civil Servants should not be permitted to participate in political discussions in your Congress.' A.G.H. Gardner-Brown (for SNA) to Nabulyato, 27 October 1948, NAZ, SEC 2/1119.

CHAPTER 5

Congress Goes to the Districts

There is a long list of people who became involved in Congress from about 1950. In the Copperbelt, we worked with Reuben C. Kamanga and Noah Sambono, of Ndola, and Lawrence C. Katilungu, Simon M. Kapwepwe, Robinson Puta and Matthew D. Nkoloma, of Kitwe. In the Eastern Province, we had Shadreck Nelson Chembe and others. Northern (and Luapula) Provinces brought in Kenneth D. Kaunda, Robert Makasa and others. Our main colleagues in the Southern Province were Jeremiah Kabalata, Job Mayanda, Edward Nyanga and Job Michello. In the Central Province, we relied on January Mumpansha, David Shimobe, S.V. Kasonde and others.[1] We encountered difficulties in penetrating some Provinces and districts owing to lack of transport and also to the Northern Rhodesia government banning our entry in some rural areas through the use of chiefs (Native Authorities) and their *kapasus* or messengers. But the chiefs were acting under duress. The reader will see that chiefs under British colonial rule *did* help the fight for Independence together with us. They suffered like all of us to bring about freedom to Zambia as we know it today. We began by turning all welfare associations into affiliated bodies. Most of these later evolved into branches of the Northern Rhodesia African Congress. When welfare societies did not exist, we gave authority for branches of the party to be formed.

I have hinted at the transport difficulties faced by Congress. During the period in question, however, some European businessmen had begun to invest in the transport industry. In the Eastern and Northern Provinces and the Copperbelt, the long-established African Lakes

---

[1] All of the above began their Congress careers as branch organisers. It was only in August 1952 that the first batch of full-time 'provincial organising secretaries' were appointed by Nkumbula

Corporation was joined by Thatcher & Hobson. In the Southern Province, there were Cavadias & Nephews, operating between Namwala and Pemba, and Jones Transport, which plied the route between Choma and Namwala. I remember several times riding on top of open lorries carrying cattle hides between Namwala and Pemba. These rides were dangerous, for the hides – and the passengers sitting on them – were always at risk of falling off the speeding lorry as a result of bumps and potholes. Since the lorries of Jones Transport were covered, they were comparatively safer to ride than the others. From Livingstone to Barotseland, there was Zambezi River Transport and the Saw Mills train, in which people rode on top of logs of timber. We still relied on travelling on foot or, to a lesser extent, by bicycle. Bicycles were still rare, for they were then imported from either Southern Rhodesia or South Africa. It was a great achievement to own one of them in those days! As General Secretary of Congress between 1948 and 1953, I had to use all these means of transport to reach various areas, districts and Provinces.

In the course of my travels, I sometimes feel foul of the authorities. On my first visit to the Eastern Province in the late 1940s, Mr. Zilole kept me out of sight of the District Commissioner, Provincial Commissioner and the Police, who had begun looking for me once they learnt I was around. When it was time for me to leave Fort Jameson, it was Mr. Zilole who took me to the headquarters of Chief Undi – whom, however, we failed to meet as he was seriously ill – and then to Katete, which by then was just a Development Centre. Fortunately, the man in charge of the Centre was none other than Andrew Dale, the son of the founder of the Namwala boma. Andrew Dale Jnr. knew me. So, at Katete, I was safe the whole day. Later in the evening, Mr. Zilole transported me to Petauke, where he made sure I boarded the Thatcher & Hobson bus to Lusaka.

I was less lucky during a trip to Kasama to meet Paramount Chief Chitimukulu (Musungu). After being spotted, I was deported back to Lusaka without having reached the chief's capital. This annoyed the Paramount Chief and turned him into a staunch supporter of Congress. In the spring of 1952, when we went to England to fight against the imposition of Federation, Chitimukulu was a member of our delegation alongside Senior Chief Musokotwane (Mulena Lishumi Namahalika) of Kalomo district, Southern Province.

The system of Indirect Rule had been introduced in Northern Rhodesia from the late 1920s. It was meant to employ local chiefs under the supervision of District and Provincial Commissioners. Under this system, chiefs (some of them not even hereditary, but handpicked) were given limited executive and legislative powers as Native Authorities. They also had local courts (Native Courts) within their areas of jurisdiction. Since both Native Authorities and Courts operated under the direction of the DC concerned, it was easy for the latter to warn the chiefs of a given area against welcoming such trouble-makers as Nabulyato and the like. As a result of the DC's instructions, the chiefs' *kapasus* would conduct searches and even arrest the accused without knowing the reasons behind the order. The chiefs were thus compelled to disregard the time-honoured African custom whereby a visitor who did not have any other host would be welcomed by the ruler of the village. Despite all these pressures, however, chiefs and headmen gradually learnt the realities of our movement and they even began secretly to invite us to visit and speak to them together with their people.

Chiefly involvement in Congress affairs, in general, and the London Delegation of 1952, in particular, shook the Northern Rhodesian government, which thought that chiefs would always assist it in its attempt to stamp out the ANC. When we returned from England, Senior Chief Musokotwane was abducted on the evening we were due to report back to our supporters in the Kabwata Community Hall in Lusaka. Although tortured by two black persons and one European in white dust coats, the Chief refused to answer their questions, to denounce the African Congress and to accept Federation. This experience made the Chief to become even more anti-British rule in Northern Rhodesia. I could not help weeping as the Chief narrated the story to me when I went to see him in the hospital after he was retrieved from the bush by the Police to which I had denounced his disappearance. As for Paramount Chief Chitimukulu, he was deposed by the Northern

Province's PC. But the people of Lubemba stood firmly behind him, and, upon the achievement of Zambian Independence, his full status was restored. The same fate befell Paramount Chief Mpezeni (Pontino Gabriel Jere), who led a second Congress delegation to England at the beginning of 1953. Upon his return to the Eastern Province, Mpezeni was deposed by the same PC who, while stationed in the Northern Province, had demoted Chitimukulu. Again, the Chief's subject stuck by him until Independence, when he was finally reinstated. Another Chief who suffered demotion on account of his support for Congress was Senior Chief Milambo (Lwando Chiliapa) of the Ushi, Luapula Province.[2] So the reader can see the role the chiefs played during the struggle and the inconveniences they had to suffer.

Money for the Congress delegations to the UK in the early 1950s came from the people. Early in 1952, for instance, Safeli Chileshe, the then Vice-Treasurer-General of Congress, and I travelled to the Southern Province to collect over £3,000 from Job Michello, in Mazabuka, and Edward Nyanga, in Mapanza. An additional £800 came from the Northern Province. This we received in Broken Hill (Kabwe) while holding a meeting of the Congress Executive under the auspices of I.B. Nkonde. Both amounts were collected within a week of our initial appeals for funds. This speaks volumes of the reality of the power of the people, which no leader can afford to ignore. The same people who told us that we could not drive the Europeans out of Northern Rhodesia because they had guns, aeroplanes and other weapons saw for themselves what the armless power of unity can achieve. Money donated for the African Congress' delegations to England showed that the people understood the party's message.

Barotseland was the one province of the colony where Congress was entirely banned by the government. The following are some of the reasons why the ban on Congress could not work effectively in the long run. First, some of the early officials of Congress, such as Mbikusita-Lewanika, Lipalile and Richmond, were Lozi. Mbikusita-Lewanika, in particular, was none other than the son of great Lozi king, Lewanika,

---
[2] Out of the three chiefs mentioned by Nabulyato, only Milambo appears to have actually been deposed, in 1953.

and would himself become Litunga in 1968. And second, while teaching at the Kafue Training Institute, I had under my care such Lozi royals and aristocrats as Henry Yeta, Mutumwenu Yeta, Ngombala Lubita, Sikota Wina, Edwin Walubita. Some of these same pupils were part of the group of students who had given me the gift of the 'Swan' pen on my resignation from the Institute. If Barotseland heard that I was the Secretary-General of Congress, could such children and their parents really be persuaded by government propaganda not to have anything to do with me and my organisation?

CHAPTER 6

Congress Delegations to London

Between 1950 and 1953, the Northern Rhodesia African Congress embarked on a sustained effort to make its anti-federal campaign known to the outside world. In Southern Rhodesia we relied on the support of such Northern Rhodesian Africans as Solomon Kalulu in Salisbury and Shadreck Soko in Bulawayo. In Cape Town, we had Mr. Chamululu. These people did not only form Congress branches among Northern Rhodesians working abroad, but they also linked up and sought to cooperate with other regional African Congresses. Our efforts yielded quick dividends in Nyasaland and Southern Rhodesia.

In the late 1940s, the London-based medical doctor, Hastings Kamuzu Banda, began to organise campaigns in Britain against the planned Federation of the Rhodesias and Nyasaland. At that time, Harry Mwaanga Nkumbula was also in the UK, studying at the University of London. The two of them joined hands to produce an influential anti-federal pamphlet.[1] This and other anti-federal writings by Banda were sent to me to Banamwaze, whence I distributed them to other parts of Northern Rhodesia, Southern Rhodesia and Nyasaland. During our visits to London, Dr. Banda acted as our host. By the time we would get to the United Kingdom, everything would have been well arranged and laid out for us. We merely had to walk in and address meeting after meeting. It was Banda who put us in touch with such British anti-colonial organization as the Africa Bureau of Rev. Michael Scott. The secretary of the Africa Bureau, Miss Mary Benson, became our close guide and workmate, helping us to liaise with the Fabian Colonial Bureau, the Anti-Slavery Society and so on. Banda not only made

---
[1] H.K. Banda and H. Nkumbula, 'Federation in Central Africa', London, 1 May 1949, NAZ, HM 70/4/49/2.

arrangements for us to meet British MPs, but also to address rallies in a number of places. I remember addressing large public rallies with Harry Nkumbula in Birmingham and Manchester. In all our meetings in the UK, our aim was to make a strong case against that Federation of the

---

Box 6: Nabulyato's First Visit to the United Kingdom

While in the United Kingdom in the spring of 1952, Secretary-General Nabulyato kept supporters at home informed of the progress of the anti-federal offensive through regular circular letters and reports. On 26 April, he wrote

'[...] to inform you that we arrived safely. We have, since our arrival, received warm receptions from various groups of friends. I wish to tell you that whatever happens in Central Africa in this matter of Federation, we are not without friends in Britain.

The Rev. Michael Scott of the Africa Bureau gives us untiring help. The Fabian Colonial Bureau, the Anti-Slavery Society are among the many people and organisations from whom Africans in Northern Rhodesia and Nyasaland have received cordial help.

The Paramount Chief Chitimukulu and Chef Musokotwane ably present the case against Federation.

We are working hand in hand with the Congress of Nyasaland together with the official deputations from both Northern Rhodesia and Nyasaland. Dr Banda is also of great help to us.

We have already addressed several organisations and MPs, as well as members of the House of Lords. [...].

Although the Secretary of State turned down our request for an interview with him before, on our arrival he asked our Chiefs to see him but they also turned down his request.

Congress Delegations to London

> *The London Conference [on Federation] has been boycotted by Africans of Northern Rhodesia and Nyasaland. Of course only the two African stooges from Southern Rhodesia are attending the London Conference. Although these two Africans are personal friends of Sir Godfrey Huggins, they have already received resolutions against Federation from the Africans of Southern Rhodesia.*
>
> *The Congress President, Mr. Nkumbula, and Mr. Katilungu and our two Chiefs, send you greetings.*
>
> *It is not a small point to remark on the kindness of the British people. You would like the Policemen of London!'*
>
> (Source: R.M. Nabulyato, 'G/S Circular – London', 26 April 1952,

Rhodesias and Nyasaland that the white settlers in Central Africa strongly supported against the wishes of the black majority.

Europeans in Central Africa did all they could to discredit Banda. They argued he was not a Malawian but either a Jamaican or an Afro-American from the USA. As Banda contemplated a return to Africa, the Europeans were working day and night to prevent him from coming back. They argued that he was not a citizen of Federation and sought to support their case by adducing that he could not speak any local vernacular. How on earth can a person speak any African language who went out of Africa as a small boy for studies? Do Boers in South Africa speak real Dutch? Those of us who know him personally can confirm that Dr. Banda has strong memories of his boyhood days in Nyasaland. Of course, I cannot claim to know him as a politician, but in Zambia he is still known by the affectionate nickname – 'The Destroyer of Federation' – which we gave him on account of the vigorous role he played in dismantling Federation in 1963. As a medical doctor, he was greatly loved by the English people. Every time they saw black people around his surgery in London, his white patients would plead, 'please do not talk to him about going back to Africa'. I am still on very good personal terms with Dr. Banda. Whenever I visit Malawi, I remind

Malawians about my old days with the 'Ngwazi'; he himself goes out of his way to make my stay in his country as comfortable as possible.

Early in 1950, Harry Nkumbula returned to Northern Rhodesia from his studies in London. Since the government of Northern Rhodesia did not offer him employment, the African Congress appointed him National Organising Secretary. He did that for one year.[2] At the annual Conference of July 1951, Nkumbula stood for the presidency and ousted Godwin Mbikusita-Lewanika. From mid-1952, I began to scale down my activities as Secretary-General of the Congress, leaving the daily running of the organisation in the hands of my deputy, George Kaluwa, and the group which I was preparing for a takeover of office from me. When elections came in August 1953, a few weeks after the hated Federation had become a reality, I decided to step down, handing over the national secretariat to my successor, Kenneth Kaunda.[3]

But this was not the end of my political career. The Ila Native Authority of Namwala immediately invited me to take up the post of manager of a local co-operative at Kabulamwanda. Since I declined the offer, Henry Lifuna Singoi was appointed in my stead. But the Ila chiefs did not relent their pressures, for they wanted help from us, the educated people. They had been greatly impressed by the performance of Moses Mubitana, a former Methodist teacher whom they were then employing as treasury clerk (later Finance Councillor). They looked to me for similar services in the district and made me a 'modern councillor' in the Ila Native Authority. Mr. Mubitana and I worked so well together in the summer of 1953 that I was eventually elected, in October of the same year, as the representative of the Ila Native Authority to the Southern Province's African Provincial Council. The first meeting of the Southern Province's African Provincial Council that I attended towards the end of the year resulted in my election to the colony-wide African Representative Council, the highest consultative body open to Northern Rhodesian Africans. In January 1954, the same African Representative

---

[2] In fact, Nkumbula only served as National Organising Secretary of Congress between January and July 1951.
[3] Nabulyato's decision may have also been dictated by his increasingly manifest inability to work alongside Nkumbula. See, e.g., K.M. Chittenden (DC, Namwala), Namwala Public Opinion Report, 2 November 1952, NAZ, SP 1/3/3.

Council was asked to elect four of its members to sit in the Legislative Council of Northern Rhodesia; I was elected alongside Safeli Chileshe, Pascale Sokota and Lakement H. Ng'andu (now Paramount Chief Chitimukulu). My appointment was not welcomed by the then Governor of Northern Rhodesia on account of my record as Secretary of the ANC, which was giving headaches to the colonial government. The elections of four African MLCs meant that the African Congress was beginning to win battles towards Independence. All four of us in the Legislative Council (LegCo) were from the ranks of the African Congress. Since there were also two European MLCs deputed to represent African interests, the African cause in the LegCo could now count on six paladins.

CHAPTER 7
Africans in the Legislative Council of Northern Rhodesia

Africans had been represented in the Legislative Council by one European, Sir Stewart Gore-Browne, since the 1930s. I have nothing but praises for him. He did his best under the circumstances of the time, and we black Africans owe him a great deal for his services. Gore-Browne was later joined by two more European MLCs entrusted with the tasks of representing African interest.

In 1948, the African Representative Council (ARC) was granted permission to elect two of its members to the LegCo. The first African MLCs were Rev. Henry Kasokolo and Nelson Nalumango. The number of European MLCs representing African interests was then reduced from three to two. In 1951, Kasokolo and Nalumango were replaced by Dauti Yamba and Pascale Sokota. While Yamba moved to the Federal Parliament at the end of 1953, Sokota was elected for a second term early in 1954 alonsgide Safeli Chileshe, Lakement H. Ng'andu and myself.

The four of us decided to divide Northern Rhodesia into imaginary constituencies. We felt it was not sufficient to rely on the representative structure laid out by the Northern Rhodesian government, which turned Native Authorities, Provincial Councils and the African Representative Council into both our electoral colleges and constituencies. We needed to make contact with all the people in the country. After all, the people who made up our electoral colleges were all paid employees within the Indirect Rule system. The members of these consultative bodies, in other words, were not free representatives of the people. They thought they were favoured by the government. They were not aware that the salaries and allowances paid to them by the government came from the people's taxes. Therefore, their views were not genuinely African, but danced to the tune of the salaries and allowances they were receiving from British administrators. Furthermore, Native Authority meetings were always chaired by the District Commissioners concerned, while Provincial Councils and the ARC were led by Provincial Commissioners and the Secretary for Native Affairs, respectively. Thus the entire political layout was meant to entrench government control. The Africans felt this system repressed their views. It was this situation that we sought to rectify by dividing the colony into four large 'constituencies', which each one of us would visit at regular intervals. Our plan was supported by such members of the ARC as Donald Siwale, Richard Chimkoko, Robinson Puta, Senior Chief Ikelenge and others. The country was divided as follows: Safeli Chileshe became responsible for the Central and Eastern Provinces; Pascale Sokota had the Copperbelt and the North-Western Provinces; Lakement Ng'andu was allocated the Northern and Luapula Provinces and Robinson Nabulyato was entrusted with the Southern Province and Barotseland.

These divisions were intended to ensure that the people, as taxpayers, had their voices and interests properly represented in the LegCo. After drawing up our plan, we presented it to the government for approval. Barotseland, however, posed problems. Faithful to its 'divide and rule' tactics, the government informed me that I would not be allowed to carry out any political activity in Barotseland, which they regarded as peaceful and opposed to radical politics. Between 1954 and 1956 I abided by the rule set out by the Government.[1] But in 1957, my three fellow African MLCs advised me to contact the Lozi Paramount Chief directly, i.e. without passing through government channels. To my amazement, I found out that the Litunga of Barotseland, Sir Mwanawina III, was more than willing to receive me. He even blamed me for having taken as long as three years to visit his province! Emboldened by this message, I finally paid a visit to Barotseland when the LegCo rose in April 1958.

---

[1] Nabulyato, however, did visit Barotseland in as early as 1955. See R.M. Nabulyato to Paramount Chief Mwanawina III, Lusaka, 28 June 1955, NAZ, HM 79/PP/1/55/10.

Following the protocol of the day, I contacted the Provincial Commissioner in Mongu. Instead of replying directly to me, the latter sent a telegram to the Secretary for Native Affairs to inform me that I was not welcome in Barotseland by the local authorities and people. I wondered which 'local authorities and people' he meant—perhaps the staff of the provincial headquarters office! Since the Litunga had told me otherwise, I was forced to ignore the PC's message. Using the travelling allowances to which my position of MLC entitled me, I requested an aeroplane to fly me to Mongu on one afternoon. On the morning of the same day, I sent telegrams to the provincial headquarters in Mongu to inform them of my impending arrival. Once I landed, I was received by the Lozi Prime Minster, the Ngambela, and some other indunas. They had been given a vanette by the Paramount Chief to take me to Limulunga, his winter capital, where he had moved following the Kuomboka ceremony of March. A District Officer was also at the airport. But despite his demand that I first visit the PC's office for briefing, I went straight to Limulunga. The District Officer sought to convince me to accept one of his messengers as an escort. I refused, to the amusement of the Ngambela. On the way, the latter remarked in Lozi: 'That young man is not sensible; he does not know you are a guest of the Paramount Chief'. We both laughed at his joke.

Upon arrival in Limulunga, I was given a bath and a cup of tea. Thereafter, I was accompanied by the Ngambela to meet Sir Mwanwina III, who rose to shake hands with me as I entered his lounge in the Palace. He then offered me a chair and we began to chat. We soon broke into personal jokes about the olden days, when the Lozi used to invade my Southern Province from time to time to replenish their herds of cattle. Throughout, we spoke to each other in English, much to the surprise of the Ngambela, who was used to serve as the 'voice' and interpreter of the Paramount Chief. Speaking about my duties as an MLC, I hinted at the difficulties I had encountered in preparing my visit. He smiled and broke into Lozi: 'Wena mwana aka', i.e. 'you are my son', meaning that a son was not requested to give prior notice when wishing to call on his father. I therefore deduced that I was really unreservedly welcome.

I stayed for three days in Limulunga, increasing the anxiety of the provincial administration in Mongu. On the third day of my stay, the same District Officer who had met me at the airport came to check on me. He also invited me, alongside the Paramount Chief, his wife (the Moyo) and the Ngambela, to a private luncheon in Mongu. The invitation was accepted. On the following day, as we drove from Limulunga to Mongu, Sir Mwanawina suddenly ordered the driver to stop. He got out of the car and, pointing at a village down the valley, told me: 'that is your village; all the people living there are Baila whom the Lozi captured during one of their raids into Namwala.' I replied, 'They are now Lozi, Sir. They can neither speak nor understand Chiila, just as Lozi residents of Namwala are now Baila who can hardly speak Lozi.' The Moyo and the Ngambela were amazed at how the Paramount Chief and I got on well together both in English and Lozi.

A 'diplomatic incident' nearly spoiled the reception at the PC's house. When we entered the residence, the Lady of the House offered chairs to everyone except me! The Paramount Chief expressed disgust in Lozi and wished to leave. I pleaded with him to wait for the arrival of the PC and, to ease the situation, I even decided to sit on the carpet! When the PC, accompanied by two of his junior officers and their wives, entered the room, he was shocked to find me sitting on the floor. He could not help showing annoyance for he understood what had happened. He apologised to me and finally offered me a chair. On the way back to Limulunga after lunch, the Paramount Chief asked me how I felt about the whole thing. I replied that that was nothing, for I had faced and was facing worse treatment than that, not only as a politician but also as a black man. I added that I accepted the PC's apology, for the poor Lady of the House had clearly not been told in advance who I was. She just treated me as she would have treated any other black man. And I also reminded Sir Mwanwina that he himself would face similar humiliations if white people met him without being aware of his high status. That, I concluded, was the general treatment given to us by all the whites. The Paramount Chief painfully appreciated the spirit with which I put up with all these inconveniences.

I remember a similar incident taking place in the Southern Province during my term as Secretary-General of the Congress. I had cycled from Chief Mapanza to one of the towns along the line of rail to catch the Lusaka-bound train. Since I was tired, hungry and thirsty, but had only 45 minutes before the arrival of the train, I went to a nearby European hotel and asked to be served a meal. The manager of the hotel brushed my request aside. Eventually, his wife agreed to feed me in the hotel's kitchen. For political reasons, I accepted the offer and ate my meal on the floor of the kitchen, paying 15 shillings for it! The lady, who had not recognized me, was not to blame, for if her white customers had seen me eating at the hotel, she was likely to lose business. The hotel still exists, so I shall not name the town where the incident took place. From these events, however, readers will have formed a picture of the unfairness of the treatment reserved to black Africans in a colonial situation.

After my stay in Limulunga, I returned to Mongu, where I lodged with the Senior Boma Clerk, Mr. Kalimukwa, a personal friend whose twin sons I had taught in Kafue. After addressing two meetings in Mongu, I proceeded to Sefula mission, where I was known to the missionaries from my days at the Kafue Training Institute. After addressing yet another meeting in Sefula, I spent two more days in Namushakendi and then returned by air to Lusaka. I think my trip to Barotseland proved how wrong the colonial administration had been in stating I was not welcome in the Province and how low it was prepared to go in the furtherance of its 'divide and rule' tactics.

CHAPTER 8

From the Split in the African National Congress to Independence

On 24 October 1958, I learnt from the radio that a splinter group from the ANC, Nkumbula's party, had been formed under the name of Zambia African National Congress (ZANC). This was the body led by Kenneth Kaunda, who had taken over from me as Secretary of the Congress in 1953. Among those who joined the new party were Simon Mwansa Kapwepwe, Congress' former Treasurer, and many others. Having been myself General Secretary of the Congress for many years, I understood the reasons for the split. Already in the early 1950s, I was merely patching up cracks which others could no longer tolerate. Therefore I was ready to go with the new organisation.[1]

In March 1959, ZANC was banned and its top leaders restricted to rural areas. One of the ZANC internees in Namwala was Wittington K. Sikalumbi, the outlawed party's Vice-Secretary-General. By the time the United National Independence Party (UNIP) was formed in the summer of 1959, I was no longer in the LegCo and was therefore ready to become a member of the new organisation. At the time, UNIP was under the interim leadership of the lawyer Mainza Chona, who stepped down to the advantage of Kaunda once the latter was released from prison.

My adhesion to UNIP was not well-received in Namwala, where Nkumbula's ANC remained dominant. Once, a Congress meeting was convened at Banamwaze, my home, with the aim of discrediting me and my family as sell outs. The meeting was addressed by Nkumbula. There was commotion; drums were beaten, and the whole of Namwala district

---

[1] Nabulyato is very unlikely ever to have joined ZANC, as attested, for instance, by his taking part in the 1959 LegCo elections that ZANC had resolved to boycott.

seemed to converge on Banamwaze. The ANC youth went berserk beating everyone they met who was not a member of their party and especially those whom they suspected of belonging to UNIP or who hailed from different provinces of the country. The boma feared for my life and sent four policemen and two messengers to guard me and my house. I chose to dismiss them, informing the boma that I was at home and nothing untoward could happen to me. People who attended the meeting realized they were being bluffed. The ANC aimed at disgracing my name, but instead it disgraced itself. It was the death coffin of Congress in Banamwaze. The ANC began doing itself self-arm by seeking to discredit other people and other organisations. As the Bemba say, 'ubufi bulabwelela', that is, 'lies turn against oneself.'[2] The African National Congress resorted to confining itself to tribalism, districtism and provincialism.

In 1960, I concentrated on home life and a small transport business. I bought two motor boats to transport people and goods on the Kafue River between Banamwaze and Namwala. Due to the presence of numerous hippos in the river, people found this to be a safer means of transport than canoes. Early in 1961, I purchased a 4 ½ ton iron boat with a custom-made canopy and inboard diesel engine. This enabled me to expand my transport business on the Kafue river. After securing hawker licences for Namwala, Mazabuka, Mumbwa and Lusaka districts, my boats began to ply the Kafue with merchandise to be sold to local fishermen. Life became so comfortable that when, in 1962, Mainza Chona visited me in Banamwaze to persuade me to stand for elections to the Legislative Council on a UNIP ticket, I declined. I told him I needed a ten-year-long rest! I added that I had already exhausted my physical and mental energies in fighting battles with successive colonial governors and travelling the length and breadth of the country.

Between 1964, the year of our Independence, and 1968, several top government and party officials sought unsuccessfully to persuade me to enter the foreign service. Among them was the then Foreign Minister, Simon Kapwepwe. Once, I was even summoned to meet the Republican

---

[2] Contrary to what is implied by Nabulyato, the Namwala Constituency remained safely in the hands of the ANC throughout the life-span of the Zambian First Republic.

President, Kenneth Kaunda, in Namwala. Despite his pressure, I emphasized that I was not interested in getting a job abroad. I added, however, that I might consider something within Zambia.

Following this exchange, I was appointed to serve on the Board of Directors of the Land Bank. At the time, with the Credit Organisation of Zambia still operational, the Land Bank was mainly catering for the needs of white farmers.[3] All of the Board members were Europeans, with the exception of five Africans: H. Makulu (the Chairman of the Board), A. Soko, U.G. Mwila, S. Chisembele and myself. I was suddenly brought back to my days in the LegCo, when it was difficult to get anything for Africans against the wishes of the majority of European members. The Land Bank tended to give loans only to people who could provide securities; in practice, this meant the European farmers alone.

One day, I decided to play it thick. We were discussing the case of a white farmer in Mkushi who had absconded to Southern Rhodesia after receiving a loan for his farm equipments from the Land Bank. Many other white farmers had played a similar game in the past. I protested to the Chairman: why continuing to give loans to people who could easily run away and go elsewhere? Why are we denying loan to Africans who are here, will die here and be buried here? Oh, the day became dark for my fellow European Board members! After my outburst, the white General Manager of the Land Bank was replaced by an African. This change of personnel and attitude now gave black farmers the chance to get their loan applications approved too. Before these events, I thought white farmers were rich. I had not realised that they owed the government millions and millions of Kwacha. Their farms, their cars, their tractors, and even the wages they paid and the food they ate had all been bought out of government funds. It must be said, however, that some of these farmers worked hard, repaid their loans and thus helped the economy of the day.

In 1965, I received a message from cabinet office to attend the African Freedom Day on 25 May. I was to be honoured on account of my past services to Zambia and be made an 'Officer of the Order of the Grand Companion of Freedom'. Sir Gore-Browne, who had been

---

[3] The hugely inefficient Credit Organization of Zambia folded in 1970.

awarded a similar honour, was also in attendance at the ceremony. I approached him to greet him. At first, he did not remember me! After I told him my name, he tried to rise and hug me, but, as he himself admitted, was too feeble to do so. I tried to cheer him up, but, in a sombre mood, he said: 'Robinson, it's time I went. The fact I could not recognise you means I am no more of this world – we may never meet again like this.' I was greatly humbled and nearly broke into tears. All I could say was, 'Sir Stewart, I am happy we are receiving this award which is a recognition of our services to this country.' He replied, 'indeed, we have done our part'. Sir Stewart did not live long after that, he 'went'.[4]

---

[4] Gore-Browne died in Kasama in 1967.

CHAPTER 9
Invitation to Take Up the Speakership

Since 1965, the year in which I received honours and awards, the government of the Republic of Zambia drew me nearer to itself. In 1966, for instance, I was invited by Justin Chimba, the then Minister of Foreign Trade and Industry, to lead a trade mission to Italy. The delegation also comprised Daniel Katungu (a Lusaka businessman), C.C. Patel (a Kabwe-based trader) and J.V. Malauni, who served as the delegation's secretary. We visited Rome, Milan and Turin, where the Fait headquarters are located. Surprisingly, Fiat cars in Italy are durable, but when they are assembled in Zambia, they do not perform to the expectations of the customers.

On 12 November 1968, after attending a meeting of the Board of Directors of the Land Bank, I went back home via Monze and Namwala, where I stopped in a shop I had recently bought from an Asian trader. This new shop in Namwala was intended to be an extension of my long-established business in Banamwaze. At about noon of 13 November, an unexpected airplane landed at the Namwala airstrip. An officer from Lusaka emerged from the plane and went straight to the boma looking for me with a letter from His Excellency the President. The District Secretary directed the messenger to my shop. The President's letter read as follows: 'I sent that plane, please come to Lusaka and see me before 4 p.m. I am thereafter leaving for London today.' Without hesitation, I put my business books aside, picked up my briefcase and left the shop for the airstrip. J. Hambulo, the District Secretary who drove us to the airstrip, joked: 'I hope this is not the last time I see you, Rob'. I replied: 'Yes, this could be the last time if the plane drops us down.' I reached Lusaka slightly before 2 p.m. and was rushed to State

House. As soon as I met the President, I was offered the job of Speaker of the National Assembly. Before I even had the chance to reply, the President said his deputy, Kapwepwe, would give me all the information I needed, for he himself was about to leave the country for the UK. Having earlier committed myself to considering the offer of a government job within Zambia, I could do nothing beside accepting the appointment.

The Vice-President instructed me to go to cabinet office, where I found out that all was set for me, including the former residence of the erstwhile Minister of Finance, Arthur Wina. Alas, on my first night, I found myself without beddings or food! I initially used my own savings to furnish the house. I only began to receive my salary and allowances in January 1969, after I was elected into the Chair and sworn in. Before that could happen, however, I had to go back to Banamwaze and inform my family of the new situation. My wife was very encouraging, but was not easily persuaded of the need to relocate to Lusaka. Instead, she elected to remain in Banamwaze to look after our business affairs in the Namwala district. This was painful for me, but I now see how foresighted she was. One problem I left unsolved in Namwala was finding a school place for my son, Godfrey, who had just ended his Grade 7 and was ready to begin Form I. Thanks to the good offices of his uncle, Isiah Mushabati, and a Catholic priest in Namwala, Father O'Connor, the headmaster of Namwala secondary school was persuaded to offer Godfrey a place in his school.

In Lusaka, I received my salary between January 1969 and April 1976, when it was discontinued on account of my owning a business in Namwala. This clashed with Zambia's socialist laws against so-called capitalists![1] From that time onwards, I rendered service to the country without drawing a salary. I, of course, continued to receive my allowances, but, after taxes, deductions, etc., these totalled a paltry K20 to K30 per day. My wife assisted me by sending me money whenever necessary. However, as a result of my long absence, our business in Namwala took a turn for the worse. The transport business collapsed in 1976, when the 4 ½ ton iron boat sank at Chonamabwe, Banamwaze. All

---
[1] This is an obvious reference to the provisions of the Leadership Code of 1976. See below, box 9.

my cattle died of tsetse fly bites in 1978, when, due to the Itezhitezhi dam having flooded the Kafue plains for longer periods than in the past, my cattle had to be kept upland, in the dry and tsetse-infested bush.[2] Mrs Nabulyato and I have been ruined irreparably by politics. Had I remained at home twenty years ago, things would undoubtedly have been different. Perhaps, as one of my closest friends once remarked, my 'reward is in heaven'. Perhaps the socialists – whom I see preaching poverty in public, but amassing wealth in secrecy – have a better clue! Upon knowing I was not receiving a salary, some kind MPs offered to help me with money, which I always refused for I have never been so desperate as to lead the life of a beggar. Some other people, who still thought I was a highly paid state official, appealed to me for financial assistance. All of these have ended up being disappointed. When people pointed out that the Leadership Code was not being applied fairly ('some of your colleagues in the Party are getting all their salaries while they own farms and big businesses with fat bank accounts abroad'), I either kept silent or replied by pointing out that I was not a cheat.

The ANC, which, as pointed out above, had earlier sought to discredit me for joining UNIP, tried to prevent my election to the Speakership. Both Nkumbula and his right-hand man, Edward Mungoni Liso, did their best to get Wesley Nyirenda, another UNIP man, re-elected to the Chair. A tense confrontation ensued during which I refused to recognize Nkumbula as Official Leader of the Opposition in the National Assembly due to his parliamentary contingent numbering only 23. In 1970, Nkumbula took the matter to the High Court, applying for an order of mandamus to be directed at the Speaker. Judges Hughes and Magnus took Nkumbula's side, despite an Act of Parliament making it clear that whatever is said and decided upon by the House is not liable to be questioned in any court or place outside the Assembly. I am not sure whether Mr. Justice Magnus, himself a former MP of Welensky's United Federal Party (later National Progressive Party), would have done the same if the person occupying the Chair had been

---

[2] The dam had begun to operate in the early 1970s. For a recent summary of the ecological disruption it brought about, see 'Dam Gives Way for Wetlands in Zambia': www.afrol.com/articles/14882 (accessed on 11 June 2007).

of his white colour. All these efforts were meant to frustrate me in my early days as Speaker.

Between 1972 and 1973, I supported the move to bring about a one-party system in the country through the merger of UNIP and the ANC.[3] This has contributed to the development of the country, even though, on the political side, life is not all that glorious. I make this remark because elections are only superficially more peaceful under a one-party dispensation than they were during the first, multi-party republic (1964-1973) Candidates are still fighting and killing each other well before general elections are held. What is different is that political bickering under the one-party state takes place in secret, whereas in a multi-party dispensation it occurs in the open. The one-party state is most suitable for developmental purposes, but the multi-party system excels for the purposes of democratic government.

> **Box 7: Fighting Harry Nkumbula in the National Assembly and in Court**
>
> Nkumbula's decision to involve the High Court in the matter of Nabulyato's refusal to recognise him as Leader of the Opposition resulted in a series of 'secret' and 'top secret' exchanges between the Speaker of the National Assembly and the Republican President, K.D. Kaunda, who, anxious to avoid a conflict between the Speaker's office and the judiciary, repeatedly asked the former to back down. When, in 1971, Nkumbula sought to repeat the trick by threatening to take legal action against either Parliament or the government over the delay in calling six parliamentary by-elections, Nabulyato could hardly contain his indignation.
>
> *'The courts and the country as a whole are being misled and I wonder how long Mr. Nkumbula should continue to mislead the Republic through the use of legal proceedings on even frivolous issues. It is my duty, as Speaker, to run Parliament and it is becoming unfortunate that the courts involve*

---

[3] To speak of 'merger' is not entirely correct, for while the one-party state bills passed by the National Assembly at the end of 1972 outlawed the ANC, with the Choma Declaration of 27 June 1973, Nkumbula and Liso agreed that 'all provincial, district, [and] area branches' of the ANC 'should forthwith identify themselves with the United National Independence Party'. The text of the Choma Declaration is to be found in the Archives of UNIP, Lusaka, ANC 9/21.

themselves through Mr. Nkumbula in trying to direct Parliamentary affairs. This will sooner or later force me to use Parliamentary instruments against Mr. Nkumbula's actions for which he will regret together with those who connive with him.

Now turning to the actual question of by-elections [...], you, Sir, advised that all the [...] vacant constituencies should be dealt with together after those in the courts were cleared. As a Member of

Parliament, instead of getting this information from my office to know where the delay lay, Mr. Nkumbula goes to other places and thereafter goes to the Press. [...].

Sir, I wish to state that there are limits to which Parliament can go in exercising tolerance over peculiar irregularities which continue to arise amounting to intentional sabotage against Parliament. It was and is most unfortunate that, in Zambia, the courts aim to indulge into Parliamentary affairs over which they are not competent merely to protect Mr. Nkumbula who fails to attain Parliamentary qualifications for recognition [as Leader of the Opposition]. [...].

Mr. Nkumbula is a salaried Member of Parliament but he chooses to be an enemy of Parliament by inviting outside institutions or forces to indignify [sic] it in addition to depleting its funds through costs on legal proceedings. [...]. The Legislature, the Executive and the Judiciary are the three arms of Government. They can differ but it is fatal if the courts can place themselves in complete isolation by causing unnecessary conflicts between themselves and other arms of Government like Parliament.

Please have a word with the Chief Justice, I request, Sir.'

(Source: R.M. Nabulyato to K.D. Kaunda, [Lusaka], 27 July 1971, NAZ, HM 79/PP/1/71/3)

During the first years of the Second Republic, UNIP MPs hailing from the Southern Province were still ridiculed as being 'Congress' in Parliament. This has now died out, to the benefit of development in Zambia. Up to now, in 1988, I consider we have done our best as a state to uphold the democratic principles of freedom of speech under our one-party parliament. Perhaps, this is a subject requiring a book on its own. Here, I only wish to comment that many African countries look to us as a successful example of one-party participatory democracy. I admit that the one-party state has both virtues and weaknesses, as has the multi-party system. There is nothing perfect in this world. But this depends on praxis more than principles. Some of the countries that have adopted a one-party democracy have fallen prey to the machinations of the party in power. Yet, no Parliament can claim to be living a democratic existence unless it is made independent of either the ruling party or government. When this is not obtaining, Parliament is made to serve dictatorial purposes. Once the party or government in power begins to resist the people's criticism or decisions through Parliament, then it becomes impossible to rule the country concerned except through the barrel of a gun.

CHAPTER 10

Parliamentary Government vs. Dictatorship

It is a fact that, in Africa, we do not realise that poverty and social backwardness are associated with instability. Those who happen to get to the top and rule other Africans always tend to cultivate a personality cult or ideology, which they exploit to thwart the people's ambitions by offering them false promises of a better and more prosperous future. Such dictators or oppressors do not like educated people around them for fear that the latter might expose the ruses they employ to rule the uneducated masses and the poor. I say this because in 1987, when I visited the USA, I found a good number of American universities and colleges being manned by African professors who had been forced into exile by cruel black African regimes, and this despite Africa being short of skilled manpower! It would thus appear that the end of white colonialism has not brought freedom to the Africans, who merely witnessed one kind of dictatorship being replaced by another. Independent African states have continued to inflict indignities and sufferings on their own people, often using the same tactics as their colonial predecessors, of which the new African rulers have tended to become the indirect agents.

African leaders use various divisive methods to cause conflicts among their citizens. They do this by calling some people 'poor' and other 'rich'. On account of this strategy, people begin to hate each other, while the master puppeteer looks on, enjoying the success of his tricks. As people fight, the ruler will now appear with an air of innocence and offer arbitration, mainly in the form of material help to one or all of the warring factions. He thus takes on the mantle of Saviour, even though he himself was the original cause of strife in society. This reminds one of the colonial strategy of 'divide and rule'. When a country has a Parliament, it is natural for its enlightened citizens to aspire to become Members of Parliament to protect the interests of the people as a whole. But tyrannical rulers will normally endeavour to have a Parliament of their own liking. The dictator in question will form a bogus political party or parties, which he will present as being entrusted with the task of defending the interests of the poor against those of the 'exploiters'. Yet, strictly speaking, it is almost impossible to find any black African who can be regarded as a capitalist or a rich person outside government circles. It is the African leaders themselves who can be called capitalists because, unlike the average citizen, they have ways of accumulating wealth. This is due to various factors, not least the lack of private capital to establish businesses and the oppressive economic policies imposed by many African leaders through the political parties they control. These policies make it difficult, if not impossible, for anyone to develop sound business ventures. In a number of cases, security organisations are set up to be used against anyone who tries to develop his business along lines that are instead appreciated in plural societies.

Some of the African exiles I spoke to in the States told me they had left their countries to make honest money. In Africa, they alleged, only dishonest persons or crooks were able to do that by evading the attention of authorities who consider the enjoyment of wealth as their exclusive prerogative. African leaders do not want to see other black men being comfortable. Really, are these not jealousies at work among African leaders? The majority of people engaged in business are simply earning a living. To call them exploiters or capitalists serves merely to prevent them from taking part in the political development of their countries. Furthermore, many dictatorships have laws that allow them to confiscate, 'in the interest of the state', businesses which have reached a certain level of profitability. In most cases, these moves are simply dictated by the political wish to deprive citizens of the possibility of getting rich. Poor people, it is often assumed, are easier to rule. But this is wrong, because rich people in the UK, the USA, Japan and other developed states do not pose their governments any special problems on account of their wealth. Such selfish policies in Africa have been and will continue to be the causes of coups d'état. African leaders are therefore advised to exchange their dictatorial attitudes and greed for wealth with a genuinely democratic mode of life.

The leaders of totalitarian states – where all criticism is silenced through various means, including the disappearance and lynching of opponents – are obsessed with protecting their own positions. They do this by misusing the taxpayers' money to surround themselves with police, army and other security forces with which they threaten and frighten away even the sensible and dignified citizens who are simply bent on providing them with good advice. As a result, these leaders become isolated from the true realities of life and turn into tyrannical dictators, examples of whom are so abundant in Africa.

Most tyrants or dictators aim at the humiliation of their subjects, for they know that 'a mean-spirited man will not conspire against anyone.' The dictator desires that all his subjects should be powerless and incapable of action. But repression only sharpens and hardens resistance. Thus, political leaders should not turn their parties or security forces into instruments of oppression. For to do so is to invite their own downfall. They should instead rely on democratic principles both in private and public dealings. A democratic leader wins the confidence of his people and does not need to go to the extent of wearing a bullet-proof vest!

A dictator is a frightened person. Thus he speaks out gloriously, but his actions are different. The signs and proofs can be easily seen. In a dictatorial state, it is enough to give a cursory glance at the size and composition of the security forces on which the dictator relies to deter potential aggressors (who include fictitious dissidents and other imaginary internal enemies). The dictator suspects everyone, except himself, of having the intention of overthrowing him. N.M. Chibesakunda and I personally saw this in Idi Amin's Uganda in January 1972. Our plane from Kenya to Liberia landed at Kampala to refuel. My word, we were not even allowed to get in the terminal building for the then ruler of Uganda suspected everyone on earth of plotting against him! There were guns and guns everywhere around the airport. We thus remained on board the plane for three solid hours. It was a hot day, and we perspired profusely as Amin's security forces searched and sprayed the aircraft with disinfectant.

A dictator is also obstinate and does not appreciate what others do under his authority. He is all the time busy hunting for faults in others so as to antagonise them. He is minutely careful and trivial in detecting mistakes in people whom he thinks are becoming more powerful than he is. He will most often devise ways and means of plucking feathers from their wings so as to prevent them from flying. He wants to be the suppliers of all things and is so totalitarian that his thinking flourishes in undermining others. This is the obsession of most leaders in Africa. Yes, this brings disaster to many African countries.

Fortunately, democracy in Zambia has not suffered any dictatorial deflections since we introduced the 'One-Party Participatory Democracy' in 1972-1973. But I cannot say what the future will hold because many a one-party state have fallen prey to dictatorship. Further, most, if not all, dictators pose as gods (human gods, of course). They thus expect people to worship and praise them in hymns. This is especially characteristic of one-party states, which are therefore viewed with suspicion by all multi-party polities. The latter argue that the one-party system militates against the 'Rule of Law' and does not permit genuine debate to take place. This, however, has not been the case in Zambia during the past fifteen years.[1]

In my understanding, the key role of a Member of Parliament, especially in a developing country, is to act as an intermediary between the people, on the one hand, and the government, on the other. When sitting in the House, an MP conveys the people's interests and views to the government. When he is among his constituents, on the other hand, he explains the government policy to the people. In the House, the MP must ensure that the laws being made are not against public interests. When debating policies, he scrutinises and, if needed, criticises the actions of the government. In doing so, he keeps the government in check against its administrative lapses. Finally, an MP controls the raising and spending of the nation's money during budget debates. But

---
[1] This statement is in manifest contradiction with the substance of chapter 11.

in Africa, due to the pressures emanating from the leaders in power, these all-important functions are not easily performed. Frequently, there tends to be a degree of conflict between theory and practice – a conflict that makes the MPs insecure and afraid to play as meaningful a role as they should.

In all democratic countries, Parliament is the highest legislative forum. In some parts of the world, however, there are Parliaments that operates as purely passive instruments for the unanimous endorsement of whatever law the ruling party or the executive might propose. Such legislatures play a very limited part in the political life of their countries and are often dismissed as 'rubber stamps'. On the contrary, in those countries where the legitimacy of Parliament is upheld, the legitimacy of government themselves depends on the authority conferred upon them by the electorate through Parliament. An institutional dispensation of this sort forms the basis of the so-called 'Rule of Law'. And since Parliaments have the right to consent to taxation, MPs should defend their right to question the actions of their governments. In one-party systems, a distinction must be made between the *policies* and *actions* of governments, for while the former might not ordinarily be opposed in Parliament, the latter do remain subject to the MPs' scrutiny. The MPs' right to criticism includes the possibility of rejecting Bills that the House considers as being solely designed to suit the interests of the ruling party, as opposed to those of the nation as a whole. When leaders in a given government begin to think of themselves as being 'great' and conceited, they are sowing the seeds of their downfall. This will be the consequence of their failure to comprehend the nature of the institutions which they themselves have created. The Romans and the British are shown historically to have been the victims of their own complacency.

The need for properly educated people to enter political leadership is obvious. If people of the right calibre do not come forward to become Members of Parliament, then the country concerned suffers, for it will be ruled by the wrong people, including the backwards and the imbeciles. Parliamentary government is not possible without the existence of one or more parties. One writer on parliamentary history has stated that 'the best brains under normal conditions of a free society, when not united by a common loyalty to a Party or committed to a Party Programme, would constantly be disagreeing and getting into loggerheads and thus failing in their duties of Government.'[2] Under revolutionary or military regimes, the role of Parliament has generally been emasculated to such an extent that membership now amounts to little more than a self-enrichment strategy. It is worthless to aspire to enter such Parliaments since all decisions are predetermined and there is no genuinely free debate based on knowledge or experience. The only Parliaments to appeal to potential members are those that do not preclude the possibility of unfettered discussion. Members of these Parliaments, which I term 'evolutionary' (as opposed to 'revolutionary'), are unlikely to be motivated by base motives. In Zambia, people sometimes say that politicians only go to Parliament to get rich. This claim, however, does not really hold water, for retired MPs in Zambia have generally struggled to make ends meet.

It is a great honour to serve one's country as an MP. No person in a country is one's own property. Each citizen belongs to the state to serve it. When its legislative powers are unlimited (rather then being despotically curtailed through government decrees), Parliament is both omnipotent and sacred, entertaining, tolerating and accommodating all shades of opinion in the nation. Thus, while political parties rise and fall, come and go, Parliament remains to receive new MPs for the service of the nation. Parliament is a power not to be ignored or belittled in any state.

---

[2] The source of this quote could not be identified.

CHAPTER 11

Parliament in the Zambian One-Party State

In the Zambian one-party system, people enter our country's Parliament if they belong to the only legal political party in the country, UNIP. The constitution of UNIP states explicitly that all members have rights and obligations towards the party. However, when dealing with an MP, it has to be borne in mind that the latter occupies a special dual role, for, besides representing party interests, he is also entrusted with the task of representing the interests of his constituents, not all of whom belong to UNIP. Article 87 of the Zambian Constitution states that 'Members of the National Assembly shall be free to speak and vote on any issue in the Assembly.' And this is reinforced by the National Assembly (Power and Privileges) Act Cap 17 of the Laws of Zambia, whose section 3 reads as follows: 'There shall be Freedom of Speech and debate in the Assembly. Such Freedom of Speech and debate shall not be liable to be questioned in any Court or place outside the Assembly.'

In a political system like ours, where we believe in the 'Rule of Law' and not in the rule of the sword and the gun, the party in Parliament (i.e., the MPs) should remain free to discuss and refine party politics without fear or favour. Naturally, since all MPs belong to one party, they are expected not to oppose their own party, as doing so would be ethically wrong. But if their criticisms are meant to ensure that the party works more efficiently for the betterment, not only of its own position, but of society as a whole, then there is nothing wrong with the MPs exercising their right to scrutinize all the arguments put forward by the party in promoting specific pieces of legislation. It is thus inevitable for MPs to be critical of party policies. Indeed, it is from such process that the Zambian system of parliamentary government draws its strength. Party members should not be offended by what is said or done in Parliament. The MPs' role as representatives (as opposed to delegates or deputies) means that they are first and foremost answerable to their electors; the party, in this regard, must come second. MPs, of course, hold their positions in virtue of the party having sanctioned their candidature. But once elections are over, the party should be expected to operate in the background in relation to parliamentary work. If we are unable to comply with this provision in Zambia, then we should not describe ourselves as a democratic state.[1]

These general rules have held firm until about 1980, but in the last few years I have observed a tendency to muzzle the freedom of speech of MPs in the House on the part of UNIP. Sometimes, the attacks on Legislators have been so fierce as to contravene the letter of Article 87 of the Zambian Constitution and Section 3 of Cap 17 of the Laws of Zambia. There are many examples that could be made, but the first that springs to mind is the public rally during which a Provincial Political Secretary referred to the MPs as 'traitors' on account of their utterances in the House. In January 1987, during the opening of one of the Fourth Sessions of the Fifth National Assembly, the Head of State berated MPs for making anti-party statements in the House and seeking to get involved in cheap polemics. He enjoined not to forget that it was UNIP that had made their election possible; he ended by asking: 'How dare the MPs now cut off their noses to spite their faces?'. These remarks infuriated the MPs, and the debate that followed President Kaunda's address was so heated that it almost divided the nation. Thank God, common sense prevailed in the end.

On yet another occasion, the state nationalized some milling companies, declaring them strategic industries. When some MPs questioned the wisdom of this move, top leaders outside the Parliament lambasted the Legislators and threatened some of them with disciplinary action if they continued to support the affected millers. And this took place despite the fact that the Statutory Instruments under which the takeovers were effected make explicit the right of unsatisfied

---

[1] These first two paragraphs consist of the editor's rendering of a lengthy letter written by Nabulyato in 1980 and reproduced as the incipit of the original chapter 14.

parties to petition Parliament. On 16 April 1987, the *Times of Zambia* wrote that the President had stated that

> Millers were so upset about the takeover and they had 'bought' some MPs to champion their case in Parliament. But he warned that should any MP take up the matter in Parliament, he would be disciplined as a Party Members for shielding 'thieves'. He said Parliament had been abused for too long.[2]

When the millers did petition Parliament to complain about what they deemed to be inadequate compensations, the National Assembly appointed some Select Committees to deal with the matter. Unfortunately, the Government saw fit to frustrate these initiatives by deciding not to summon Parliament. One can only regard this as a method for killing democracy. However, in spite of these threats and pressures, Parliament went ahead and, faithful to the letter of the Laws of Zambia, heard the petitions through its Select Committees.

I have always believed that democracy can thrive in a one-party state if Parliament is allowed to operate in an atmosphere of unfettered freedom of speech. While an MPs owes allegiance to his party and government, he is not to be turned into a puppet deprived of real powers in the House. He must remain as free as his fellow human beings outside the walls of the House. In my ruling from the Chair, I have on many occasions appealed to the ruling party to tolerate some of the MPs' pronouncements for the sake of democracy. In a ruling dating to as early as April 1978, I was forced to point out that the Press was contributing in three ways to creating a rift between the party and the National Assembly:

1. by publishing dead issues or matters ruled out of order during debates with a view to inciting undue animosity;
2. by reporting unfairly on debates, e.g. by printing the criticisms of Government on the part of some MPs and leaving out counter-arguments and governmental replies;
3. by keeping silent on the good work carried out in the House and concentrating solely on the mistakes committed

---
[2] 'KK rejects "dirty" money: state to buy mills at book value', *Times of Zambia*, 16 April 1987.

by MPs and especially by the big names in the latter's ranks. This brought about unnecessary hostility among party cadres and divided the nation into camps.

Often, Parliament is depicted by the Press as an imaginary enemy of the Zambian revolution. I continued to point out that the role of the National Assembly is to legislate, vote money and debate. During its debates, the House gives expression to the mind of the people, teaches the nation what the nation does not know and makes the people hear what they would not otherwise hear.

Freedom of speech for MPs is the pillar of any parliamentary democracy. Without it, democracy is dead and dictatorship stands ready to fill the vacuum thus created. From the foregoing, it would appear that some of the reasons that led us originally to bring about a one-party system are becoming less and less cogent. Dictatorship is showing its face around the corner, and even inter-party violence, a significant feature of the first, multi-party republic, it raising its head again during the clashes between supporters of opposing election applicants. Clashes of this nature were reported from the Copperbelt and Livingstone in September-October 1988.

Box 8: Nabulyato on the Role of Parliament

Speaker Nabulyato was always a strong defender of the prerogatives and independence of Parliament. His stance acquired a manifest political significance in the 1980s, when the one-party Parliament often served as an outlet for the voicing of widespread concerns about the increasing unpopularity and isolation of the real seats of power in the country: the Executive, the Central Committee of UNIP and, of course, the Presidency. In the twilight of Kaunda's rule, the most outspoken and foresighted UNIP MPs in the National Assembly and Speaker Nabulyato himself came to be viewed by many as fulfilling the functions of an 'unofficial opposition'. This is the context within which to place the following – guarded and yet courageous – speech, which the Zambian press read as a defence of the right of the MPs to criticise the government (see, e.g., *Times of Zambia*, 7 June 1987)

'Hon. Speakers and Presiding Officers, I now like to turn to the important business for which we have been meeting these last few days. [...]. As Speakers and Presiding Officers, we speak for Members of Parliament who are the spokesmen entrusted by the people with the task of expressing the views of the public and the wishes of the population to the Executive: our main duty is to listen and occasionally to guide the proceedings of the House. [...].

Hon. Colleagues, I also wish to remind ourselves of the fact that Parliament does not govern and is never intended to govern. Parliamentary Government, often spoken about regarding democracy, does not mean Government by Parliament. Rather it means a strong executive government tempered and controlled by constant representative criticism. This is the idea at which Parliamentary institutions aim. However, this should be jealously guarded especially in single party Governments because, as the bonds of Party discipline tend to tighten, the one and only political party in any given state can become an instrument of repression on the citizens or taxpayers through Parliament enacting oppressive laws which meet the desires of the Party. On this point, multiparty system excels the one party type of Government in keeping the political views balanced. Of course, according to our experiences, the one Party system is best suited for Developing countries. However, the business of Parliament is threefold for which rights, privileges of immunities and freedoms of speech are provided: these are legislative, financial and critical. Where there is no Parliament or once Parliament gets controlled by outside forces, a country automatically becomes a dictatorship as opposed to what is generally cherished in democracy. [...]. I appeal therefore that wherever there is Parliamentary Government in the Commonwealth countries, democracy should be practised according to the framework of the constitutional provisions of each individual State concerned [...]

I appeal to all Houses of Assembly, Houses of Representatives and Houses of National Assembly in the Commonwealth of the Africa Region that they should allow the State to govern through Parliament.

This is the basis of democracy. The duty of Parliaments is to provide mutual avenues for a two-way traffic, viz:

a) Parliament controlling the Executive, and

b) The Executive governing through Parliament.

[…]. It is a fact that most Governments, if not all, in the world prefer Democracy to Dictatorship because Democracy is an art which allows people to discuss and give consent to being governed by the State authority to which they pay taxes, so as to maintain services and to develop the country. Therefore, it would only be a mummified ruling party in any State, be it multiple or single party, which would usurp the authority of the people by claiming the promotion of development of a country without giving due credit to the citizens, whether party or non party members, who support national coffers through Parliamentary Representative sanctions. […].

We in Zambia have coined Democracy with an adjective "Participatory", making it into "Participatory Democracy", indicating that in the One Party we introduced there was all the room for all people to participate in running their government. It is, however, important to remember that political parties come and go but Parliamentary democratic systems remain: of course, some parties serve democracy well and others just spoil it. Hence, we Speakers and Presiding Officers should continue to remain independent and never take sides when occupying the chair of the House. We are all aware that if one, in the Chair, came from the Ruling Party, the Party would expect and even pressurise support from the Chair. However, our part is to protect even the minority or lonely voice in the debates of the Houses of Parliament. […].'

(Source: R.M. Nabulyato, Farewell Address to the 'First Conference of Commonwealth Speakers and Presiding Officers in the African Region', Lusaka, 5 June 1987, reproduced *in extenso* in the original version of 'African Realities', chapter 10, NAZ, HM 79/PP/10/5)

CHAPTER 12

The Spirit of Self-Help and Sacrifice in Zambia and Africa

My experience of the spirit of self-help and sacrifice in Zambia are very favourable, especially when appeals from the government to the people are not too onerous and frequent. Calls for self-help and sacrifice do not backfire when they are occasional. Too frequent appeals, on the other hand, become boring, especially if the Government is not contributing its own share of resources to complement the independent efforts of the local communities concerned.

In colonial Zambia, the missionaries who brought education and medical care to the rural people never had to put up schools or clinics or the houses for their teachers and medical workers. These were built by the villagers, who appreciated the services rendered on to them. The colonial government, too, drew upon self-help, especially when 'Native Courts' were built in many chiefly capitals from the late 1920s. Even when permanent material were required, the local people provided the bricks, while the government gave them the corrugated iron sheets, doors, windows and so on. In Namwala, in the 1960s, Moses Mubitana and I mobilised the people of the district to donate towards the building of the University of Zambia. Their willingness to give was beyond description. But, if they are not to antagonize tax-payers, these appeals cannot continue ceaselessly.

It appears that after Independence in 1964, some of the services that the people had provided for free were taken for granted by the state. And in the 1970s, the Zambian government, more and more unable to contribute to the various projects promoted by local communities, began to request the latter to start and complete their initiatives without any additional assistance. While educated Zambians appreciated that this was due to the economic malaise that beset the country, the uneducated rural people were disappointed by this change of policy. Today, whenever rural Zambians hear their leaders calling for sacrifices and making appeals to the spirit of self-help or self-reliance, they fail to understand. They even ask such questions as: 'We pay numerous and heavy taxes, where do these leaders take all the money?'; 'When the colonialists were in Zambia, we paid few and light taxes. We were then happy to provide services to the government. Today, however, we are still asked to make sacrifices and to resort to self-help even though we are contributing heavily to government's coffers through our taxes and donations. Where does all this monetary sacrifice go?' And they add that 'everything the Europeans left behind is deteriorating and no renovations are being carried out.' Governments in Zambia and Africa as a whole take days, weeks, moths or even years to address these questions.

Voluntary self-help and sacrifices can provide development only up to a point. African governments should employ a mixture of self-help and paid-for-services to boost development. Such a combination would provide a more meaningful service to the people. People do not eat rhetoric but food. People cannot live by education and civilisation alone; they need wealth and prosperity. Poverty is the source of all evil. Thus, leading a people or a country into poverty is the most inexcusable sin any human being can inflict on mankind and fellowmen. A rich man can afford to be generous, whereas a poor man is cruel, for he is always planning how best to steal from the rich whom he sees as an exploiter.

African people in the villages have their own autochthonous self-help or self-reliance programmes. These could be studied and utilized for achieving a higher level of development. Instead, many African leaders alienate their people by inviting them to join exotic schemes they do not understand. It helps to realise that people appreciate schemes that start 'from the known to the unknown' (as a teacher would have it). Many African leaders are not sufficiently attuned to the ideas of their fellow countrymen. If they were, they would not invite foreign ideologues to instruct their people. And while the latter are spending time coming to terms with new and foreign theories, precious time for development is wasted! Sometime, coercion has to be employed to force the people to accept such foreign dogmas. The political leaders who subscribe to foreign ideologies end up being alienated from their people and, by using counterproductive development strategies, they commit

---

Box 9: Nabulyato on the Leadership Code

Nabulyato's pro-business orientation and obvious fatigue with UNIP's mismanagement of the Zambian economy and trite sloganeering emerge quite clearly in a long letter he wrote to Malimba Masheke, the newly appointed Prime Minister, at some point in 1989. Although the letter exists only in draft form, and it is not clear if it was ever sent, it is indicative of the author's critical political position during the last years of UNIP's rule.

'Although belatedly, I write to congratulate you Sir on your appointment as Prime Minister in our Government. [...].

2. On ... 1989, I wrote to your predecessor Mr. Kebby Musokotwane MP asking him to repeal the Leadership Code as well as reviewing most if not all Government policies in Zambia which vex people for nothing. These arebecoming obsolete or are unAfrican. The Leadership Code has proved a mockery as it is an instrument of Apartheid among leaders in the Party and Government. It depicts [sic] foreign cruelties of Stalin's Russia and Mao's China. [...]. Zambian leaders made carbon copies of policies from Socialist or Communist countries. As a result many countries in Africa which have done likewise have had to spoil and damage their own States. Zambia in particular has suffered for <u>nothing</u> over the past 25 years of her Independence. We have adopted policies to starve and torture people without thorough study as to whether or not policies based on <u>deprivation</u> are suitable to African conditions. Hence we have followed "hollow policies of praising poverty and despising wealth or riches." [...].

3. Mr. K. Musokotwane's reply to me revealed lack of understanding of economic-politics. He discussed Humanism which is irrelevant to economics. He also added that people not prepared to comply with the

> *Leadership Code should decline accepting office of leadership when called upon. [...]. If normal people resolve to decline appointments as advised by Mr. K. Musokotwane, shall we not be ruled by imbeciles and ill educated people or is this the aim of Government in Zambia to use fools who cannot see beyond their noses? [...]. Please repeal the Leadership Code. It is encouraging corruption in Zambia as it forces Leaders to do business secretly.*
>
> *4. [...] I am myself a victim of the Leadership Code. My experiences show how the Leadership Code is mostly responsible for the damage of the Zambian economy. It kills pride in people to boost the economy through their individual efforts as opposed to co-operatives which merely encourage consumption by lazy wide mouths. [...]. Because of the Leadership Cod, almost <u>all</u> leaders in the Party and Government of Zambia are engaged in underground or secret business of one kind and another [...]. Children of Leaders act as agents or fronts of their parents' multi-national companies both in Zambia and abroad flouting the Leadership Code. [...]. It is today an open secret for people to seek re-appointment to their former posts if they are suspended or sacked [...]. Yes, Zambia has been economically weakened by some people who know "how to play it safe for themselves." These Mr. Prime Minister are things you are herein asked to watch out. Many fictitious events are mysteriously talking place under swindles conducted by prominent people in safe or privileged positions in the corridors of power. These are also quick to harass other people on petty offences leaving big money untalked [sic] about. I am conveying all these to the Government through you Sir so that effects of some laws like the Leadership Code can be clearly seen as to how back-firing these are on the State. [...].'*
>
> (Source: R.M. Nabulyato to M. Masheke, n.p., n.d. [but mid-1989?], NAZ, HM 79/PP/1/89/1)

the same mistake that colonial rulers incurred into. Leaders themselves are not always to blame, for many of them have not grown up among the people and do not understand indigenous modes of life. But the fact remains that a black Europeanised or 'Asianised' leader cannot deliver development in an African context. The adoption of foreign political systems and ideologies in Africa sets the clock back. And while some leaders boast about the peace, stability and unity they are promoting, their states sink into debt or dismal poverty. One, then, is forced to conclude there was something basically wrong from the start: forced peace, stability and unity cannot create prosperity and wealth in any country. People must be free to acquire wealth by working for it in liberty and in an unmolested environment.

The noblest achievement for any nation is Independence. However, during my over fifty years of public life, I have remarked that, all over the world and especially in Africa, this noble achievement is often abused by those who assume authority. This is because once a person is elected to lead the people, he adopts a holier-than-thou attitude. He thinks of himself as the wisest citizen in the state and forgets that all the power he holds ensued from the sacrifice of the people who fought for freedom and liberty from the colonial yoke. I have visited many African countries whose leaders have turned against the very people who placed them in positions of authority. These leaders regard some citizens as 'enemies' of the state who should be eliminated. When people realized that it had been their own sacrifices and efforts that had put these same persons in charge, the latter found themselves overthrown. It is unwise to regard citizens as internal enemies. This wholesale condemnation of people is repugnant. This, however, is something we have not witnessed in Zambia, and it is helpful to realise how fortunate we have been in our country in having good people as leaders. On the basis of my political career and experience of world affairs, I feel that Zambia has had something special to offer to mankind.

I have visited several countries in Africa, Europe, Asia and America where people are employed by the state to go about planting troubles and causing fights among their citizens. Once problems are created, then the ruler of the day takes pleasure in governing by chaos and terrorism. Such misuse of the opportunity of self-rule has brought about a return of dependency. In Africa, we see countries getting so ideologically colonised that foreign powers are even invited to come and fight their wars! I have also visited many African countries where civilians have been declared redundant, their only function being to pay taxes through which to fund the growing security apparatuses which the leaders use to protect their ill-gotten positions. Citizens of these latter countries are deprived of freedom, while soldiers and other security forces go about inflicting violence on their fellow countrymen instead of protecting them against their external enemies. And even people living under such oppressive conditions are requested to work hard to be self-sufficient and self-reliant! It is common knowledge, today, that the leaders of most of Africa tend to be blind to world events. These leaders continue to misuse the standing armies under their command by turning them into instruments of repression.

Lest I am misunderstood, I wish openly to appeal to Africa to be more liberal and democratic than it has been since Independence. A number of countries in Africa have done well, but some others have shown themselves to be as cruel as white South Africa. Because of this, Amnesty International is doing a commendable work in fighting against torture and for the defence of human rights in Africa and all over the world. Men of goodwill should rally behind this organisation which is fighting a worldwide war for a noble cause. Jails are bursting with prisoners, some of whom are detained without a trial for months and years, just because dictatorial regimes want to intimidate alleged internal opponents. In some African states, honesty is a waste of time and energy, for an honest man can be made to suffer unfairly in the same way as a rogue or an anarchist. I appeal to African states that practise oppression and torture to abandon their repressive policies for democratic and human forms of rule.

I have written some hard things about African leaders. I do, however, wish to state that, in Zambia, we have tried to follow the principles of a Christian state, and I think we have not done too badly under President Kaunda. In Zambia, I am one of the architects of the one-party state. And up to now, I am satisfied with the democratic way in which it has operated.

The Spirit of Self-Help and Sacrifice in Zambia

> **Box 10: Human Rights' Abuses in Zambia in the 1980s**
>
> Despite his open professions of loyalty to UNIP, Nabulyato was well-aware of the extent to which human rights' abuses were rampant in Zambia in the 1980s. Under the Preservation of Public Security Regulations, President Kaunda could order the incarceration without trial of virtually every opponent of UNIP. One of the latter was Alfred Musonda Chambeshi, about whose plight another detainee, John Chipawa Sakalunda, wrote in the summer of 1988
>
> *'I wish to inform you that Ba Tata Ba Shikulu Chibale is still ill in bed at Kansenji State Prison as he is not feeling well after collapsing on 11th July 1988 at about 11:00 hours just after he had gone to our nearest clinic within the vicinity of the Prison premises for clinical treatment as he had been complaining of general body pains on Sunday just before our evening lock-up.'*
>
> (Source: J.C. Sakulanda to various members of the Chambeshi family, Kansenji state prison, Ndola, 12 July 1988, NAZ, HM 79/1/PP/F7.)
>
> After receiving Sakulanda's letter, the Chambeshi family sought to enlist Nabulyato's assistance to secure the release of the aged and sick prisoner.
>
> *'I am authorised by the family of Mr. Chambeshi to write to all his friends and acquaintances to seek their moral support and assistance in asking His Excellency the President Dr. K.D. Kaunda to release him on compassionate grounds.*
>
> *Mr. Chambeshi is about 70 years old. When he went into "preventive" detention over a year ago, he was already hypertensive and a sufferer of stomach ulcers. Subsequently, he became so ill he had to be hospitalised in Ndola Central Hospital. His Doctor even wrote a Report on Mr. Chambeshi's medical condition and this Report was sent to State House together with a letter from Mr. Chambeshi's family, pleading that at least he be placed into restriction at his Mkushi Farm. This letter was never replied to or acknowledged. [...].*

> *As members of his family, we are duty-bound to request the assistance of any humane people or organisations. Your esteemed Parliament is one such organisation. We ask Parliament through your good offices, Sir, to speak to K[enneth] K[aunda] on our behalf in the most conciliatory way possible, so that by the President's kind considerations, we may be spared an untimely funeral of our beloved Parent.'*

(Source: Abel M. Chambeshi to R.M. Nabulyato, Lusaka, 25 July 1988, NAZ, HM 79/1/PP/F7)

CHAPTER 13

The Economic and Political Future of Africa

Africa looks like a question mark on the world map. The continent faces a very uncertain future because of the policies and actions of its leaders. I do realise that African countries have great future potential for development. But are leaders helping to foster it? The Zambian situation allows some room for optimism. Our achievements in less than twenty-five years have been fantastic, especially if one bears in mind our meagre resources and poor economy. The schools, hospitals, roads and other infrastructures we have built speak volume, but are we clear about our future direction, or are we working to leave debts and mortgages to posterity?

In some African countries, elections are rigged as a matter of course. The use of security forces, corruption and intimidation falsifies the outcome of electoral contests, leading to the election of leaders of low calibre and poor quality. In 1986, I visited one African country during its ruling party's annual conference. Two candidates took part in the elections for the post of party chairman. Two ballot boxes were provided, but, on election day, only the box of the favoured candidate was left open; the second box remained sealed throughout the proceedings! I could not believe my eyes, but there it was. Fearing reprisals, the voters, including the supporters of the victimized candidate, found it impossible to speak out against the rigging. The same applied to the election officers, who just went through counting the votes in the open box and the few ballot papers scattered around the sealed box. A good number of frustrated voters just tore up their ballot papers in the polling boots and pocketed the pieces. During successive meetings, no one bothered to stand against the party's preferred candidate, who thus continued to be returned unopposed. As an official guest, of course, I could do or say nothing. But this episode made a lasting impression on me. In Africa, it is rare to have someone winning an election or being returned unopposed without 'dirty tricks' being employed. But where can such leaders take Africa who were elected through dubious and treacherous means? Most African governments are shaky because they are based on such sandy foundations.

Corruption extends well beyond the electoral sphere. African leaders and their families get involved in scandals without any sense of shame and, instead of stepping down, would rather continue to govern with a bad name. Some are said to be billionaires with fat bank accounts in foreign countries. With such rumours circulating on the continent, Africa gets a bad reputation and its leaders are not taken seriously when they remind the world of the structural problems they are contending with. There are countries which have fallen into trouble with the International Monetary Fund or the World Bank because of the fallacies of their leaders. Corruption in high places is a cancer, and as long as Africa's leaders keep on helping themselves to loans, donations and grants meant for public use, a dark cloud will hover over the continent's future. It is corruption that has caused many African leaders to lose all international respect. Such actions on the part of African leaders frustrate progress and development. People read of an African leader's son being sentenced to prison for smuggling jewels or drugs; of some central bank's money mysteriously going missing; and of the children of African presidents being at the head of large business empires without having ever worked to raise the required funds. And the leader whose honesty is thus called into question remain unperturbed in office! But his corruption outlives him, and when he dies, his family is made to account or suffer for it.

Because of corruption in the handling of loans, donations and grants, donor countries and lending institutions no longer trust African leaders and now insist that the fate of their money and the projects for which it is to be used be closely monitored in loco. What this means, in practice, is that the experts that accompany Western money come to Africa to earn it back for their own countries. When the experts leave, of course, the projects they have implemented cannot be adequately managed by Africans who, being excluded from the preliminary phases of the projects, have not acquired the necessary skills and expertise. And loans have to be repaid. When one takes stock of all of this, it is difficult to be optimistic about the future of Africa's economic recovery programmes.

Where is Africa going? Do African leaders see the way or are they just drifting in a ocean, being pushed by the winds and leading their peoples nowhere? People fought for independence to be free, not only politically, but also economically and socially. But many African leaders are cruelly denying these forms of freedom to their people by depriving them of the means to acquire wealth and education. When Britain began granting independence to her African colonies, beginning with Ghana in 1957, many African countries were deprived of the necessary educational skills to manage their affairs. In fact, most, if not all, of the newly born African states became too excited and never thought of doing first things first. Each country on the verge of independence had to – in Nkrumah's words – 'seek [...] first the political kingdom'. The hope was that everything else would follow suit, including the 'economic kingdom'. But the new leaders inflicted economic slavery on their people by adopting foreign ideologies as tools with which to govern their countries. Many African countries began drowning one by one and went bankrupt as a result of their love for foreign ideologies. Ushering in the nationalisation of the economy, these ideologies resulted in the people being deprived of the means to earn an independent livelihood. Private enterprise was sabotaged and everyone was reduced to looking to the government for everything. By the time African leaders realised that private enterprise sustained more people than governments ever could, unemployment, starvation and misery had already set in.

A state-led economy produces more thieves than honest citizens. Dirigisme also saps individual initiative. It is said that 'a watched pot never boils'. When controlled and closely watched, workers will not do their best. They will, for instance, not work on a building in manifest need of renovations until ordered to do so. Those appointed to positions of responsibility must be given room to work according to their training or skills. They will then do wonders. Despite its equalitarian and redistributive aims, the nationalisation of the economy has produced opposite effects in most African countries. Essential commodities are either astronomically priced or scarce, because people do not produce them for fear of their governments, which do not seem to want to see their citizens prosper. State monopolies produces poverty, starvation and suffering among citizens, not all of whom can be employed in the public sector. It is absurd to hear calls for self-reliance emanating from the same people who have destroyed their economies by thwarting the people's ambition to grow wealthy!

Nationalized economies have not removed inequality; rather, they have consolidated the position of privileged minorities who enjoy plenty in the midst of mass deprivation. Where there is continuous famine, fatness denotes power. While the populace wear rags and live in slums, the privileged few wear gold and build mansions or palaces. Such inequalities, of course, cause profound antagonism; the populace hate the wealthy, and the latter fear the former. Many African countries are said to be poor. Yet their leaders are rated amongst the richest men on the planets.

To put it bluntly: almost all African countries are failing to grow economically because they have copied or adopted ideologies which are either irrelevant or inappropriate to the real needs of their citizens. It is all a fallacy. If one gave a sum of £1 each to, say, fifty people and came back after a certain period, one would find that while some recipients would have spent all the money given to them, others would have saved a little or even invested part of the original £1 with a view to earning more out of it. Having a free mind and aspiring to independence, these latter category of people would in all probability be antagonized by their government. African governments want ignorant and poor citizens who clap in praise of their fallacious theories and dance for their meals from the state. African leaders throw their fellow citizens in prison until the wealth of their victims is ruined. This is the 'political kingdom' for the

African rulers who rejoice at inflicting sufferings on other people. Of course, no African leader would ever admit this. They are in high and comfortable positions. They have forgotten the pangs of hunger for their daily meals are assured by the taxes paid by the people they oppress.

It is important for Africans to be aware of the fact that capital will always be needed. Many new countries in Europe, Africa, Asia and Latin America believe that the way to bring about socialism is to fine, persecute or even liquidate their millionaires. To justify such moves and the requisition of the wealth of its victim, the government concerned would normally accuse the wealthy of 'having stolen. How else could they manage to accumulate such patrimony in their life time?'. This line of thinking is cheap and criminal, to say the least. People work and save or invest to accumulate wealth. It is not true that all rich people are thieves. Rather, they are the people who are able to put to good use their individual initiative and willingness to work hard. Ignorant rulers need to understand this. More often than not, the real thieves and exploiters are the rulers of the so-called socialist governments of Africa and the world.

In some socialist countries I have visited, the rich have been killed to nationalise their wealth. These same countries now have veritable ghost towns, whose once beautiful houses are falling into disrepair. Real socialism is predicated on the even spread of wealth that can be achieved by producing and justly remunerating skilled labour. Blind or cruel socialism, instead, mismanages a country's economy and causes poverty among its citizens, for all the wealth is concentrated in the hands of the rulers, their followers, wives and relatives. This is the main reason why African leaders like and accept socialism. But the conditions that brought about socialism in Europe are not applicable to Africa. Besides, even in today's Europe socialism is falling to pieces to be replaced by democracy. So, why adopting something alien to Africa? Socialism goes hand-in-hand with cruelty and ungodliness.

One particular feature of African politics militates against the continent's future development. While some African leaders limit their terms in office, others wish to hold on to their positions until they are

Box 11: Nabulyato on the USSR

Nabulyato's deep-rooted hostility to Communist regimes and to the attempt to import some of their policies into Zambia inform his confidential 'Report on Zambian Parliamentary Delegation to Moscow, USSR: 27th July – 5th August, 1977'

'This Report is confidential for I intend to make it critical of some situations we observed. [...]. I dare have to report that our observations show that USSR is basically a poor and badly organised country. [...].

a) Basic Poverty of USSR

Food production is far too low for the 260 million people. Industrial development is placed in some areas for political appeasement and convenience as opposed to distances of Raw Material Production. Only 16 million people who are Members of the Party eat and sleep well, especially those in Moscow in the Russian Republic who happen to be the Ruling Class. Although there are 15 Republics in USSR, the other 14 Republics (apart from the Russian one) are mere agents of meagre production of food and raw materials for consumption in Moscow. [...]. This also explains why USSR imports food even from her enemy-countries like USA.

b) Bad Organisation of USSR

The Communist Party in USSR caters mainly for 16 million people who are its Members. The rest out of the 260 million people fend for themselves which means living in dire poverty and starvation as the cream of production and consumption is under control of the Party. Life is therefore miserable in some areas away from centres of big cities or Development Created Centres. In other words, the bulk of the people in USSR starve or are left to the mercy of supplying cheap labour and exploitation under the guise of voluntary service to the State. Those among the 16 million people enjoy life and for them the slogan "it pays to belong to the Party" really means life. Those living in Moscow City [...] are the cream or Ruling Class in USSR. They are a lazy and arrogant lot. [...]

The Economic and Political Future of Africa

> *It is advisable to be cautious about [the USSR]. This is because USSR is drunk with being a Big World Power so much so that all their thinking, actions and talks are centred on organising, planning, plotting and manoeuvring coup d'états, riots and confusions in other parts of the world so that they can sell, give and intervene with their powerful weaponry and other helps which they supply to other countries with <u>Strings</u> attached. [...]. Further, although USSR may have no colourbar, there is in USSR a "Lookdown" attitude on people from the Third World and Africa in particular. USSR aim and wish are to confuse or colonise Africa by use of their Ideology-indoctrination and Money in order to make African States as sources of food and raw materials as well as finding room for Strategic Bases for USSR.[...]*
>
> *Undoubtedly, the Soviet Union has become a Big Power in the World but a Starving Nation under their Socialism. Our visit to Lenin's Study and Flat in the Kremlin revealed the tenacity and simplicity of Lenin as opposed to how a number of leaders in the Eastern Bloc live, work and behave. The Soviet people starve because they spend huge sums of money on Big Power Maintenance and on Non-productive constructions of imposing buildings, monuments and statues. [...].'*
>
> (Source: R.M. Nabulyato to K.D. Kaunda, Lusaka, 25 August 1977, NAZ, HM 79/PP/77/5)

either incapacitated by old age or dead. Experience shows that those who step down while still fit are honest leaders. Having realised their own limitations or failures, they now wish for others to have a go at leadership and to seek to restore the pace of economic development. It appears that, in most cases, leaders of this kind have nothing to hide. The leaders who refuse to relinquish power, on the other hand, are often convinced of being popular and argue that they would step down only if their people asked them to do so. This is self-deception springing out of conceited thinking. Some may feel that, by stepping down, they would be seen as cowards running away from the errors they committed in the economic management of their countries. In practice, these leaders think they are indispensable.

African leaders never examine their conduct and shortcomings, let alone being open to criticism. Instead, they tend to place the responsibility for every problem on the shoulders of a long-gone colonialism. Almost all independent African countries are fast becoming dictatorships, since anyone who dares criticizing their leaders is immediately dubbed a 'dissident' or an 'anti-party element'. This is true of both one-party and multi-party regimes. Even constructive criticisms are seen by African leaders as insults that deserve to be punished. As a general rule, shortly after independence, most African countries began to dismantle their democratic institutions and to consolidate the powers and status of their executive presidencies. Today, it is as difficult to get rid of an autocratic president as it was to replace a despotic colonial governor. Afraid of becoming 'nonentities' upon their retirement, most African presidents cling on to power. But the more they stay in power, the more unpopular they become. And their unpopularity, in turn, increases their dependence on repressive methods. Presidents, of course, also seek to consolidate their hold on power through co-optation, i.e. by giving a share of the spoils to feebleminded civilians. The latter form a moneyed elite group of loyalists. But popular dissatisfaction with tyrannical black regimes is growing by the day. Several strikes, riots and revolts are taking place in present-day Africa.[1]

---

[1] Major food riots had rocked Zambia's urban centres in 1986

CHAPTER 14
Threats to Democracy in Africa

My discussion of Africa's future would not be complete if mention were not made of the role of standing armies on the continent and its implications. During the last decades, coups d'état have been a common occurrence in Africa. In some country, the armed forced have taken over the government machinery out of their own initiative; in others, they have eagerly responded to pleas from the people or the politicians, especially in situations of a complete breakdown of law and order or when economic problems were threatening the very existence of the people. More often than not, after usurping power, the soldiers have humiliated, tortured and even executed their civilian predecessors. Or the latter have been thrown in jail for the 'crimes' they are accused of having committed while they were in power.

It is fear of such eventualities that has led most African leaders to seek to appease their countries' armed forces. Most African governments profess to be democracies and should therefore treat the military like any other component of the state bureaucracy. The armed forces, in turn, should press their claims through the prescribed channels and comply with the ultimate decisions of their superiors, the civilian authorities. But this has not been the case, for the majority of African leaders have, out of fear, chosen to turn the military into a special class of people, submitting meekly to their every wish and bringing them close to the centre of power. The result of these manoeuvres is that the armed forced develop corporate pride and confidence, both of which translate into a still greater degree of influence. But, as the old adage has it, 'familiarity breeds contempt'. Eventually, the civilian leadership is so weakened that the armed forces begin to disdain it and to plot a takeover. Military coups are the result of the short-sightedness and selfishness of African leaders. When people suffer, they are more than happy to accept a military regime. They argue that all dictatorships are the same, whether civilian or military. The only way for a civilian leader to prevent this state of mind from setting in is to operate democratically by upholding constitutional rights and freedoms.

Up to now, it is true, Zambia has enjoyed uninterrupted peace and political stability. Yet, when I take stock of realities on the ground and think about the future, I shudder. Zambian leaders, in particular, do not

---

Box 12: Nabulyato on the Risk of a Military Coup in Zambia

As shown by the following, secret letter to a beleaguered Kaunda, Nabulyato's anxiety about the possibility of a military takeover in Zambia in the late 1980s was far from academic.

'Your Excellency,

Ever since Auction was introduced in Zambia which has resulted into increased prices in all areas coupled with widespread unemployment, tensions have been rising in the country against the Leadership to such degrees that all sections of the population are now losing confidence in the Zambian Government. [...].

[C]ivilians today are secretly demanding [sic] in their conversations that Leaders are bluffing the country. That it is the leaders themselves who have ruined the economy – that leaders' children both males and females are Presidents and Chairmen of not only millionaire Conglomerates in Zambia, but also of multinational Companies all over the world. Conversations in public places have it that Leaders must bring back the money they have either taken out to other countries or hidden in their children who have become Billionaires without having worked for nor earned the money. People are today mentioning names in the Leadership which is a real danger especially that even Security Forces no longer confide in the Leadership. [...]. Arguments are that if Zambia continues with One Party System,

there must be a forced revolution through Military action to overthrow the Government even if this be unconstitutional so that people are freed [sic] from starvation and from the whims of the few in the One Party Leadership where huge sums of money have been spent on Security for fictitious or imagined wars and to protect the few in the Leadership. [...].

[S]ome suggestions are that to avoid Soldiers from taking over:

a) There should be appointed a Commission of Inquiry to examine the successes and failures of the One Party State System in Zambia.

b) That the Commission of Inquiry be headed by a Supreme Court. [...].

c) That the Commission of Inquiry be composed of 12 members, 3 of whom should represent the Central Committee and the rest outsiders or ordinary citizens including soldiers if they wish to take part. This will foil any military plans for a coup which is now allegedly eminent underground. Retired soldiers are behind the move as they feel misplaced since some of them know of no other fields of training or work from being Soldiers. [...].

d) That Central Committee be dissolved and an Interim Central Committee appointed. People think the Party UNIP is dying quietly. Only salaried Party men keep it, the rest of the so-called UNIP members

do not believe in it any more than giving it lip service. No one can profess this openly but it is unfortunately circulating invisibly.

e) That the present Parliament be prolonged for 1 year and thereafter conduct elections on a new

Constitution as the present one will have been amended. If the Military takes over early, then this thought will have been overtaken by events.

The suggested proposals are meant to combat the coup by the inclusion of Military and other Security Forces into the new system in a different form than now. [...].

The situation that obtains in the Nation worries me Sir because all appears quiet on the surface but deep down, from what reaches my office, all is not

> well Sir. [...]. All these Sir, coupled with heavy taxes, make Military coup a real possibility and welcome step as far as Zambians are concerned today. [...].
>
> Your Excellency, I have submitted these frank disclosures and recommendations or suggestions in the spirit of national unity or interest. None of us would like to see the country plunged into chaos as such a thing would only lead us to unnecessary bloodshed and even dragging the country several years backwards. Sir, it is often stated, "Prevention is better than cure." Hence this letter.'
>
> (Source: R.M. Nabulyato to K.D. Kaunda, Lusaka, 31 March 1987, NAZ, HM 79/PP/1/87/1)
>
> Less than two years after Nabulyato wrote his letter, former Zambia Army Commander, Lt. Gen. Christon Tembo and several others were arrested and later charged with treason for allegedly plotting a coup.

seem to realize the dangers of delegating to the military basic policing responsibilities. Take, for instance, the case of the campaign against black marketeers in the mid-1980s, during the course of which much brutality was displayed and innocent and law-abiding citizens were harassed. What puzzles people is that the excessive powers bestowed upon the security forces have not at all contributed to finding a lasting solution to a problem that, in the ultimate analysis, has clear economic roots, stemming as it does from the scarcity of basic commodities. Only the adoption of economic policies which create wealth and abolish scarcity can reduce the extent of black marketeering. Conversely, to apply a military solution to an economic problem is both absurd and dangerous. It may well lead to the inception of a military dictatorship in such ethnically diverse a country as Zambia. The consequences of such a regime change would, alas, be too ghastly to contemplate.

The worldwide economic recession has deeply affected Africa and the living standards of her people. Some countries outside Africa have taken positive actions to improve their economies. In some cases, unproductive organisations or institutions have had to be abolished or curtailed. Armies and other state security apparatuses have not been spared. Unfortunately, instead of adopting similar measures, many African countries have continued to increase the size of their armies and even created additional security organisations. This is not because they are being threatened by hostile foreign countries, but because the military is being employed for repressive internal purposes. But armies only exist to defend and promote peace in any given country. They are not meant to ensure the perpetuation of the rule of one person or group of persons, who employ foreign ideologies to impoverish the masses while enriching themselves.

The growth of African armies has led to the proliferation of such posts as Generals, Lieutenant Generals, Major Generals, Field Marshals, etc. Yet there have been no wars to fight! However, when political meetings are convened, the armed forces turn out in great numbers! Yes, the African armed forces are well politicised, but have forgotten their prime duty of defending the whole nation irrespective of party affiliations. In the absence of external wars, taxpayers are disturbed by the incessant rise of military expenditures, which, in many African countries, even exceed state investments in such capital projects as are meant to create employment for the people. It is only by avoiding such misuse of public funds that our continent can be saved from its present economic tribulations, social and moral decay and political instability.

At independence, most African ruling parties formulated high-sounding manifestos. Unfortunately, after only a few years in power, these have generally been sidelined or abandoned to the advantage of one '-ism' or another. But this merely served to disguise the extent to which the barrel of the gun, rather than ideology, had become the prime source of the power of Africa's rulers. The future of Africa thus looks bleak. Perhaps, the continent will only be saved when a firm and genuine commitment is made to upholding the Rule of Law, and the dignity of man and parliamentary democracy. It has been said that 'African leaders are a black replacement of the colonialist with worse living conditions for the average African.' However unpalatable, this statement is difficult to refute. So dismal has the failure of African leaders been that some citizens of independent African states are even calling for a return of the former colonial rulers.

In their original constitutions, most independent African states incorporated such fundamental individual rights as the right to freedom of opinion and expression. This, of course, is particularly relevant when discussing the role of the press in independent Africa. Apart from disseminating news and educating the public, the press provides a crucial link between governments and their charges, monitoring the actions of the former on behalf of the latter. It is therefore crucial that the press remains free from any kind of government interference. This, however, does not apply in Africa, where newspapers are generally expected to take on a propagandistic role and to serve their 'master'.

Since they consider themselves as the embodiment of the state, African ruling parties exert all sorts of pressures on the press. Journalists and the thinking public are made to live in fear – fear of losing one's job, fear of being investigated and fear of being detained without trial. The nationalisation of newspapers is also a common strategy employed to gag the press. In light of all of this, it is not surprising that African newspapers tend to air only those views that are favourable to, or supported by, the government of the day. Any criticism of government policies is censored and suppressed. The result is that the press does not work as a safeguard against tyranny. Since African governments directly control what gets published in newspapers, the latter resemble *Government Gazettes*, full of government orders and decrees and deprived of real news or entertaining and educative information. Today, because of the frequency with which the freedom of the press is encroached upon by governments and the risks faced by the journalists who take their job seriously, there are very few capable, educated and experienced Africans who are prepared to work for newspapers. Civic education is the first casualty of this situation. But African leaders do not mind, for their aim is precisely to keep their countries' citizenries ignorant.

The independence of the judiciary, one of the pillars of democracy, is also under constant threat in Africa. According to the letter of the Zambian Constitution, the country's Chief Justice and the other Supreme Court Judges are appointed directly by the President. However, when appointing High Court Judges, the President is requested to seek the advice of the Judicial Service Commission, which consists of the Chief Justice, the Attorney-General, the Chairman of the Public Service Commission, the Secretary to the Cabinet and one additional member selected by the President himself. The assumption, of course, is that both Supreme and High Court Judges are selected on merit, not on the basis of their relationships with the appointing authority.

Most former British colonies have similar constitutional provisions relating to the appointment and security of tenure of magistrates as those included in the Zambian Constitution. However, in their daily functions, members of the judiciary have been far less independent than their countries' constitutions would appear to suggest. Incidents have occurred where High Court judges have been dismissed from their posts for passing judgments unfavourable to their governments or where manifest biases have been displayed in the handling of cases involving governments. Throughout Africa, the independence of the judiciary has been curtailed by tying the judges' remunerations and conditions of service to those of ordinary civil servants. To the contrary, in all the countries where the independence of the judiciary is practised in any real sense, the judges' salaries and conditions of service are determined by independent Commissions, which tend to adopt the view that the members of the judiciary should be paid at such level as to make them impermeable to bribery and corruption. In Ghana, for instance, the President of the Bar Association has recently openly accused local judges of accepting money in exchange for passing favourable judgments.

At times, even the Zambian courts are seen to have unfairly sided with the Executive. In 1986, in an attempt to curb the smuggling of essential commodities, the Zambian government introduced the Preservation of Public Security (Amendment) Bill with the view of bringing so-called 'economic sabotage' under the rubric of public security. The Bill in question was defeated in Parliament, largely because it was felt that the term 'economic sabotage' was not adequately defined and was thus open to misinterpretation. As time went by, some suspected smugglers were apprehended and charged under the Preservation of Public Security Act, Cap 106. When their cases came up for trial, some High Court judges ruled that the smuggling of such essential goods as mealie-meal and cooking oil could not be considered as representing a threat to public security. Other High Court judges took the opposite view. It was then left to the Supreme Court to pass a final ruling on this contentious point. In a lengthy and unsurprising judgment, the Supreme Court ruled in favour of the government's preferred interpretation. Without wishing to disrespect the prerogatives of the judiciary, it is necessary to point out that, though judges are competent and fully qualified to deal with disputes, it is inappropriate for policy issues to be determined through the gamble of adversary litigation. Lawmaking on political or sensitive issues should be left to the elected legislators, who, unlike the members of the judiciary, are accountable to the voters.

The independence of both the press and the judiciary are essential safeguards against tyranny. Without it, one sees nothing but darkness for these important institutions in Africa. African countries are notorious for violating fundamental human rights despite the latter being enshrined in their constitutions. Cases of detentions without trial, arbitrary arrests and suppression of freedoms of speech and religious association abound. If the press and the judiciary were to act independently and complement each other, the African record on human rights would improve greatly, and a new era of social, economic and political development be fostered.

www.ingramcontent.com/pod-product-compliance
Lightning Source LLC
Chambersburg PA
CBHW01071730042 6
44114CB00021B/2879